Personal Discipline

A Biblical Study of Self-Control and Perseverance

"A Woman's Guide" series
—Revised Edition

Rhonda H. Kelley

NEW HOPE
PUBLISHERS
Birmingham, Alabama

New Hope Publishers
P. O. Box 12065
Birmingham, AL 35202-2065
www.newhopepublishers.com

Library of Congress Cataloging-in-Publication Data

Kelley, Rhonda.
  Personal discipline : a biblical study of self-control and
perseverance / Rhonda H. Kelley.
    p. cm.
  Rev. ed. of: A woman's guide to personal discipline.
  Includes bibliographical references (p.   ).
  ISBN 978-1-59669-256-5 (sc)
  1. Christian women--Religious life. 2. Self-control--Religious
aspects--Christianity. 3. Christian life--Biblical teaching. 4.
Self-control--Biblical teaching. I. Kelley, Rhonda. Woman's guide to
personal discipline. II. Title.
  BV4527.K4422 2011
  241'.4--dc22
                        2011008825

ISBN-10: 1-59669-256-1
ISBN-13: 978-1-59669-256-5
N104127 • 0611 • 2M1

~ TABLE OF CONTENTS ~

Many years ago, God taught me a profound spiritual lesson. While I was teaching a ladies' Bible study on the fruit of the Spirit (Galatians 5:22–23), He showed me that self-control was necessary to develop the other virtues. I was enthusiastic about experiencing love, joy, and peace. But God convicted me (the Bible teacher) that I could not be fruitful without self-control. What a shock! I had always thought I could pick and choose from that list of virtues. No. The fruit of the Spirit "is" the collective group of those virtues. So without self-control, there is no love, joy, and peace.

I wrote about my life-changing revelation in a book titled *Divine Discipline: How to Develop and Maintain Self-Control* (Pelican 1992). It is my personal testimony plus spiritual insights about the pursuit of personal discipline. Now this book is an interactive Bible study based on those same biblical principles. I pray that God will profoundly impact your life as you learn about His divine discipline.

You may be hesitant to begin this study because self-control is a tough topic. Few people choose to examine the subject of discipline because we don't want to be disciplined. But I challenge you to commit yourself to complete this study. I encourage you to examine the Scripture. I beg you to admit your failures. And I pray that you will trust the Lord to enable you to live a disciplined life. There is no greater blessing than a fruitful life—a disciplined life which is filled with love, joy, peace, patience, gentleness, goodness, faith, meekness, and self-control.

Divine discipline has impacted every area of my life. It continues to enable me to develop personally, grow spiritually, and serve faithfully. It is my prayer that you will persevere in divine discipline and receive the harvest of righteousness from the Lord.

—Rhonda Harrington Kelley

~ INTRODUCTION ~

Discipline may be considered by many to be a dirty word. No one wants to talk about something so difficult to accomplish. But personal discipline is essential to productive living and spiritual growth. Few teachers teach about discipline and few preachers preach about it. But God is not silent. The Bible says that discipline is a key to the fruitful Christian life. It is time for Christians to consider the topic of personal discipline and learn to practice it in our daily lives.

This Bible study contains 12 lessons that examine personal discipline and suggest steps for developing a disciplined lifestyle. It is a topical study including Old and New Testament passages as well as interactive application. I have used various resources to prepare this study, in addition to personal illustrations. Now you must make a personal decision to complete the study and apply its biblical principles to your own life. It is your first step of discipline. I recommend the following steps:

1. **Commit to discipline.** As you begin this study, you must be convicted by God of the need to be disciplined. A Bible study is meaningful only when you determine to do it and you apply God's Word to your life. Renew your commitment to discipline every day and don't get discouraged. A genuine commitment is essential to personal discipline.

2. **Decide to study discipline.** Your personal discipline will begin as you set aside time to study the topic of discipline. You can complete this Bible study on your own or as a part of a small group study. Though there are many different topics available for study, an examination of personal discipline will impact other areas of your life and promote godly living.

3. **Gather resources.** This Bible study book will be a helpful resource for your study of discipline, but you can benefit from

additional resources too. Select a Bible translation that you are familiar with or gather several translations to reference. (This Bible study uses the Holman Christian Standard Bible unless otherwise noted.) You can refer to the numerous resources listed in the back of this book for additional study. And you can find additional resources on your own.

4. **Study and apply the Scripture.** Each lesson in this book will focus on a specific aspect of discipline. You will examine numerous Scriptures about discipline, seeking to interpret their insights.

   Read the passages carefully, study their meanings, and apply their truths in your own life. Each lesson encourages personal response and includes a Scripture focus (titled "Divine Instruction"). The selected key Scripture is excellent for Bible memory and meditation. Each lesson should take 30–45 minutes to complete. You can finish the lesson in one sitting or complete sections over a period of time. It is designed for weekly study over the course of 12 weeks.

5. **Discuss discipline.** This study was designed for individual study, to be completed personally. However, discussion will make the study more meaningful. If you are participating in a small group Bible study, you will benefit from the insight of others. God can teach you through them. If you are doing the study alone, take time to discuss what God is teaching you with a family member or friend. Learning is enhanced as insights are exchanged. A group teaching guide is provided in the back of the book for leaders of small groups who wish to study this book.

6. **Share your commitment to discipline.** It is important to share your heart commitment with the Lord. Though He knows your thoughts and feelings, the Lord is blessed to hear your desire for discipline. Prayer, conversation with the Father, will support your Bible study. You will also want to share your commitment to discipline with other believers. They will strengthen you with words of encouragement

and personal accountability. You should also be compelled to share your pursuit of discipline with unbelievers. A disciplined life can be a powerful witness to others. Speak freely about your desire for discipline and give glory to God for any of your accomplishments.

7. **Continue to be disciplined.** Anyone can be disciplined for a moment. But God desires His children to be disciplined for a lifetime. So you must continue to pursue personal discipline. The completion of this Bible study is simply the beginning of the process. You must continue to be disciplined, keep on pursuing divine discipline. As you develop a disciplined lifestyle, you will bring honor to God and receive rewards for faithfulness.

8. **Enjoy the blessings of discipline.** A disciplined life is a blessed life. God will pour out His blessings on you now and for all eternity as you practice divine discipline. Though discipline is not easy, it is fruitful. You will benefit personally and spiritually from divine discipline. And you will experience great freedom in the disciplined life. Every disciplined believer can claim "very great and precious promises" to be enjoyed here on earth and experienced for eternity in heaven (2 Peter 1:4).

May God teach you divine discipline as you study His Word and experience His power!

Lesson 1
The Importance of Discipline

Divine Instruction
*No discipline seems enjoyable at the time, but painful.
Later on, however, it yields the fruit of peace and righteousness
to those who have been trained by it.* — Hebrews 12:11

Discipline is certainly not a popular topic of discussion. It seems that few people are comfortable imposing discipline on others, and even fewer relish having discipline imposed on them by others. But discipline is necessary. Parents must teach it to their children. Adults must learn it for themselves if they desire to be productive. Discipline is an important learned behavior. It is not caught; it is taught.

For the Christian, discipline is not optional. It is essential for obedient living. The Bible commands the follower of Jesus Christ to be disciplined. In 1 Timothy 4:7–8 we read, *"Discipline yourself for the purpose of godliness; for bodily discipline is only of little profit, but godliness is profitable for all things, since it holds promise for the present life and also for the life to come"* (NASB). Believers need self-control in every area of life—physical, mental, social, and spiritual. It is imperative for spiritually mature believers to develop and maintain self-control in their lives.

But wait, you say, we live in such an undisciplined world! Yes, that's true. Yet discipline is possible even in these undisciplined times. Christian discipline comes not from the strength of the person but from the power of the Holy Spirit. And though it takes hard work and requires personal sacrifice, discipline is worth it. It yields great rewards here on earth and for all eternity.

Discipline is important for many reasons. To motivate us to pursue discipline, let's focus on its importance.

Why do you think it is important to develop discipline? List several reasons in the space provided.

_____

_____

_____

Self-discipline is necessary in our personal lives, in our relationship with God, and in our relationships with others. Without discipline, we cannot grow and mature. Without discipline, we cannot experience the complete power of God in our lives. Without discipline, we cannot minister effectively to others. If we are not to falter in our Christian walk, we must develop self-control. Discipline is essential for personal development, for spiritual growth, and for Christian service. Let's examine the Scriptures to understand why discipline is important and how it influences these areas of our lives.

Personal Development

It is true that we live in an undisciplined world! People who lack discipline often suffer greatly because of it.

- Many people are **unfulfilled** in their lives because they lack discipline. They may never graduate from school or complete a project or accomplish a goal. Notice the short length of employment among workers today.
- Other people are **unaccepted** in society because of a lack of self-control. They may abuse substances or fixate on a particular behavior or unleash their rage on others. Notice the dramatic increase in road rage and airline rage in our country.
- Some people are **unguarded** in their convictions because of a lack of discipline. They may read steamy novels or wear revealing clothes or watch pornographic television. Notice the prevalence of sensual programs and commercials on television.

Personal discipline is necessary for people to develop and mature into healthy adults. Jesus Christ is the perfect example of a disciplined life. It is recorded in the Gospels that _"Jesus increased in_ *wisdom and stature, and in favor with God and with people"* (Luke 2:52). Even though He was God incarnate in flesh, Jesus needed to grow personally as He moved from childhood to adulthood. **Why do you think it was important for Jesus to discipline Himself for personal growth?**

_____

_____

Jesus modeled for His followers many aspects of the Christian life — godly living, servant leadership, and self-discipline. His disciplined lifestyle helped Him grow in wisdom and lead His disciples to be disciplined. He is our best example of a disciplined life. One New Testament translation actually says, *"Jesus kept increasing in wisdom"* (Luke 2:52 NASB). Just as Jesus kept on growing personally, we must discipline ourselves personally every day of our lives. A lifestyle of discipline should be the sincere goal of every believer today.

Every two years, countries participate in either the Winter or Summer Olympics. Television broadcasts the competition among these skilled athletes. They have disciplined themselves for years to reach a great personal goal. They have dreamed of medals and breaking records. And they have paid the price to represent their countries. Personal commitment and faithful practice are required to ensure excellence. Usually the most disciplined athlete wins the prize. As a result of sacrifice and pain, the winner claims the medal of honor.

While freedom and discipline have come to be regarded as mutually exclusive, freedom, in fact, is the final reward of discipline. Freedom is to be bought with the high price of self-discipline, not merely claimed. In her book *All That Was Ever Ours*, Elisabeth Elliot discussed the reward of a disciplined athlete. The professional athlete is free to perform in competition only because he has been, as she says, "subjected to countless hours of grueling work, rigidly prescribed, and faithfully carried out. Men are free to soar into space because they have willingly confined themselves in a tiny capsule assigned and produced by highly trained scientists and craftsmen, have meticulously followed instructions and submitted themselves to rules which others defined." It is only with dedicated discipline that true freedom is found. Freedom results from the practice of necessary disciplines.

These same principles of discipline apply to students. One of the joys of teaching is observing the personal development of many students. Often, students begin classes with deficient skills and limited experience. As they study and complete assignments, their personal growth is measurable. One of our older students in the Women's Ministry Program panicked when she was required to write a book review. She worked hard and took her assignment seriously. She wrote that first book report with great effort and pain. But, she did her work well. By the time she graduated, the student was helping others write their book reports. Her discipline was of benefit to herself personally and to others.

Have you ever disciplined yourself sacrificially to accomplish a goal?

_____

If so, how did your self-discipline affect you personally?

_____

_____

Are you a different person today because of the discipline you practiced? Explain how.

_____

_____

My husband and I were required to practice discipline as we pursued degrees in higher education. Each of us worked long hours for years to complete our dissertations. Doctoral studies are intense, and we worked on degrees at the same time. We needed discipline for the extensive research, endless writing, and the dreaded oral defenses of our dissertations. Though at times we were tempted to give up, we disciplined ourselves and encouraged each other until both doctorates were completed. Both of us learned from the process and our marriage was strengthened. The self-discipline learned from that experience has enhanced many areas of our lives.

Discipline is necessary for personal development. And personal development involves many areas of life—mental, physical, spiritual, and social. Just as Jesus increased in wisdom and stature, in favor with God and man, Christians today must be self-controlled in all areas of life. Discipline is also necessary for spiritual growth and Christian service.

Spiritual Growth

Spiritual growth is not the result of dreams or wishes. If spiritual growth is the goal, self-discipline must be developed in order to reach it. Spiritual growth demands daily discipline and selfless sacrifice just like physical discipline for the athlete does. In his book *Rebuilding Your Broken World*, Gordon MacDonald wrote about the need for regular discipline: "Spiritual discipline is to the inner spirit what physical conditioning is to the body. The unconditioned athlete, no matter how naturally talented, cannot win a world-class race." The undisciplined Christian, no matter how sincere, cannot achieve spiritual maturity. Self-discipline is necessary for Christian maturity and abundant life.

The Apostle Paul carefully discussed the fruit of the Holy Spirit in Galatians 5:22–23. He listed nine virtues of a Spirit-filled Christian. **Read Galatians 5:22–23, then write below the nine specific descriptors of the fruit of the Spirit.**

Disciplined Virtues	Undisciplined Behaviors
1. _____	_____
2. _____	_____
3. _____	_____
4. _____	_____

5. _____   _____

6. _____   _____

7. _____   _____

8. _____   _____

9. _____   _____

Love is the first in the list of nine fruits of the Spirit, followed by joy, peace, patience, kindness, goodness, faith, and gentleness. The Christian virtues are mentioned repeatedly throughout Scripture. Paul the Apostle teaches about spiritual disciplines in all his epistles. Earlier in chapter five of Galatians, Paul encouraged *"faith working through love," "serve one another through love,"* and *"love your neighbor as yourself"* (Galatians 5:6, 13-14). These virtues are considered fruit which are produced in a disciplined life.

Self-control is the last in the list. It has been described as the crowning fruit of the Spirit or the virtue necessary for all other virtues. Therefore, without self-control, there is no true love, joy, or peace. Without self-control, there is no real patience, kindness, and goodness. Without self-control, there is no genuine faith and gentleness. In fact, a lack of restraint often distorts these behaviors. **Alongside the "Disciplined Virtues" you noted above, write an "Undisciplined Behavior" that may result if there is no self-control. Take a few moments to confess any ungodly behavior in your life.**

Self-control is a pivotal fruit of the Spirit. It is the Christian virtue that enables all other virtues. Love without restraint becomes violent passion. Joy in excess is indulgence. Peace in the absence of self-control is passivity. Kindness becomes weakness, and goodness becomes self-exaltation without discipline. Faith without self-control is distrust, and gentleness to the extreme is timidity. Self-control is the fruit of the Spirit necessary for spiritual growth in a believer's life.

Simon Peter challenged believers to diligently add to their faith other Christian virtues. In 2 Peter 1:4–11, he listed seven qualities to be added to faith: goodness, knowledge, self-control, endurance, godliness, brotherly affection, and love. These virtues are marks of spiritual maturity in the believer. They are products of discipline. Self-control is a Christian virtue essential for spiritual growth.

Read 2 Peter 1:4–11, then explain why Christians must add qualities of righteousness to their faith.

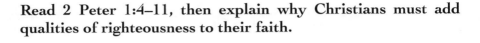

_____

_____

_____

Christians who are diligent in their daily lives will bear fruit. They will experience abundant rewards both here on earth and forever in heaven. Peter vividly described the reward of discipline in terms of the ancient Olympic games. The athlete's home city proudly welcomed back the winner through a newly opened gate in the city wall rather than the usual gate. The believer should live a disciplined life so that *"entry into the eternal kingdom of our Lord and Savior Jesus Christ will be richly supplied to you"* (2 Peter 1:11).

I am so grateful for my faith in Christ and my promise of heaven. However, I also want to enjoy the blessings of my salvation here on earth and be of service to the Lord. Therefore, I understand that I must discipline myself spiritually to build on my foundation of faith. As I devote time to prayer, Bible study, ministry, and witnessing, my Christian virtues develop. I grow in love, goodness, godliness, endurance, and knowledge as I practice self-control. My spiritual discipline helps me become more like Christ.

Richard Foster, author of *Celebration of Discipline*, concluded that Christians must sacrifice the time necessary to study the Bible, to pray to the Father, to witness to others, and to minister to the needy. This personal sacrifice of time and energy results in spiritual development. Spiritual discipline is for a definite purpose — spiritual growth. Personal development and spiritual growth are reasons for a Christian to be disciplined.

Christian Service

Discipline is essential for personal development and spiritual growth. However, did you know that self-discipline is also a prerequisite for Christian service? Lives are so busy today that daily discipline is necessary for ministry to others. Christians may think about things to do for loved ones or desire to help the needy, but Christian service will not take place without personal discipline.

The New Testament describes the life of a committed servant named Dorcas. She did not simply recognize the needs of the widows and discover her spiritual gift of ministry, she did something to help. She sewed clothes for those women who were alone. Acts 9:36 says, *"She was always doing good works and acts of charity"* (emphasis mine). Dorcas not only desired to minister to others, she disciplined herself to do it!

Are you like Dorcas or are you like me? Many times I think of helpful things to do for others or I want to minister in a particular way, but I never get around to doing it! The Bible says that Dorcas not only thought of good deeds, she did them. So, we need to be like Dorcas, disciplined in our Christian service.

Can you recall recent thoughts you have had about helping others? Have you seen needs and intended to respond? Have your thoughts and ideas turned into action? Discipline yourself to be a Dorcas! Be full of good works and loving deeds which you are always doing.

With the empowerment of the Holy Spirit, believers today can discipline themselves for Christian service. Self-control is also a qualification for spiritual leadership. In his letter to young Timothy, Paul discussed the attributes of a pastor, of deacons, and even of deacons' wives.

An overseer, therefore, must be above reproach, the husband of one wife, self-controlled, sensible, respectable, hospitable, an able teacher, not addicted to wine, not a bully but gentle, not quarrelsome, not greedy—one who manages his own household competently, having his children under control with all dignity. (If anyone does not know how to manage his own household, how will he take care of God's church?) He must not be a new convert, or he might become conceited and fall into the condemnation of the Devil. Furthermore, he must

have a good reputation among outsiders, so that he does not fall into disgrace and the Devil's trap.
—1 Timothy 3:2–7

It would be impossible even for the greatest man to meet these qualifications of a pastor without self-control. Have you ever been a part of a pastor's search committee? I have. What a challenging task! As our committee began its search for a pastor, we made a list of ideal qualifications based on Scripture. After reviewing that extensive list, we concluded with a laugh that perhaps even Jesus would have a hard time becoming pastor of our church. The role of spiritual leader has such awesome responsibility that personal discipline is required. Effective Christian service results only from self-control and Spirit-control!

Paul continues in 1 Timothy 3 to discuss qualifications of other spiritual leaders—the deacons. Most evangelical churches today select deacons to assist the pastor in doing the work of the church. According to Scripture, deacons must be *"worthy of respect, not hypocritical, not drinking a lot of wine, not greedy for money, holding the mystery of the faith with a clear conscience"* (1 Timothy 3:8–9).

Now read the qualifications for deacons' wives, women serving the Lord alongside their husbands. Fill in the blanks that follow in 1 Timothy 3:11. As you write each descriptor, remember the discipline required for spiritual leaders to live godly lives.

Wives, too, must be _____ _____ _____,
not _____, _____, _____
in everything.
—1 Timothy 3:11

Spiritual leaders can only serve effectively when they live godly, disciplined lives.

The Bible records the life stories of godly women who disciplined themselves for Christian service. In addition to Dorcas, women like Peter's mother-in-law (Luke 4:38–39), Martha (John 12:1–2), and Phoebe (Romans 16:1–2) practiced personal discipline in their service to others. The opposite is also true. Women with little self-control were unable to serve the Lord productively. Their sad stories are also included in the Bible. Eve's poor self-control hindered her influence on her own family and others (Genesis 3). Lot's wife lost her very life when she could not keep herself from looking back on the destruction of Sodom and Gomorrah (Genesis 19: 24–26). Their lack of self-control limited their usefulness on the earth as well as their blessings for all eternity.

Self-control is an essential quality for usefulness to the Master. Paul illustrated the importance of self-control to Christian service in 2 Timothy 2:20–21:

Now in a large house there are not only gold and silver bowls, but also those of wood and earthenware, some for special use, some for ordinary. So if anyone purifies himself from these things, he will be a special instrument, set apart, useful to the Master, prepared for every good work.

Personal discipline is required for useful service that brings honor to the Lord. The challenge for Christians is to be like gold and silver vessels, useful for the Master.

Personal discipline is important for many reasons. Among the motivations for self-control are personal development, spiritual growth, and Christian service. But there are many more reasons for you to practice discipline. In fact, abundant blessings are received by those who live a disciplined life.

Read Hebrews 12:11, which reminds all believers of the blessings of personal discipline. Write that verse in your own words below.

_____

_____

_____

Now, try to memorize these words as a promise to those who practice divine discipline: *"No discipline seems enjoyable at the time, but painful. Later on, however, it yields the fruit of peace and righteousness to those who have been trained by it"* (Hebrews 12:11). Remember that God has the power to help you gain control of your life! Then you can expect personal development, spiritual growth, and Christian service to result.

My Personal Discipline

Reflect on your own life. How disciplined are you? Has your self-control resulted in personal discipline, spiritual growth, and Christian service? List some evidences of your self-control below. In what ways has your discipline been useful?

Personal Development_____

_____

Spiritual Growth _____

_____

Christian Service _____

_____

Thank God for your usefulness and ask Him to cleanse you of any unrighteousness.

Dear Lord:
Convict us today of the need for self-discipline in order to develop personally, to grow spiritually, and to serve faithfully. Amen.

Lesson 2
The Essence of Discipline

Divine Instruction

*But the fruit of the Spirit is love, joy, peace, patience, kindness,
goodness, faith, gentleness, self-control. Against such things
there is no law.* — Galatians 5:22–23

Though self-control is not a popular topic or desired behavior in our culture, self-control is a necessary discipline for productive living. Before a discussion of how to develop self-control, let's explore what it means. What is self-control? What is its essence or essential components? Definitions of self-control can be both subjective or objective, personal or impartial. Self-control has different meanings to different people.

Before we examine some authoritative definitions by other people, **search for yourself for a personal definition of self-control or self-discipline. Write a definition in your own words as you complete the following sentence.**

Self-discipline is

_____

_____

_____

You may have struggled with an honest definition of self-control because it is so difficult. The disappointing consequences of poor self-control are often so painful that they overshadow the truth of self-control. As you understand what self-control is, you will be able to better develop it and continue living a disciplined life. Let's look at the meaning of self-control from a variety of perspectives.

A Dictionary Definition

One of the most helpful steps in Bible study is the searching process. If you look up something and find the answer, you will understand it better and remember it longer. So, before I give some definitions of self-control to you, take time to find some definitions on your own. **Search a dictionary or even the Internet for definitions of self-control. Write several definitions below and cite your source.**

Self-control is _____

_____

Self-control is _____

_____

Self-control is _____

_____

In my search through dictionaries I found one unhelpful definition: "Self-control is control of self." While that is a true statement, it isn't very helpful. It breaks my third grade English teacher's cardinal rule. Mrs. Brown said, "Never define a word with the word itself." I have remembered that guideline for years. So, let me share a few other more helpful definitions.

According to *Merriam-Webster's* dictionary, self-control is "the ability to restrain one's impulses or expressions of emotion." Another popular dictionary says self-control is "control exercised over oneself or one's own emotions, desires, actions, etc." The Collins Dictionary defines self-control as "the ability to exercise restraint or control over one's feelings, emotions, reactions, etc." In *Roget's Thesaurus,* self-control is "the keeping of one's thoughts and emotions to oneself." The Free Online Dictionary says self-discipline is "the act of disciplining oneself and one's conduct, usually for personal improvement."

Several common themes appear in each of these definitions of self-control. **Please reread the definitions above then note below any recurring words or concepts.**

_____

_____

_____

Do you better understand the meaning of self-control?

Self-control is definitely a behavior—a deliberate action, the ability to act. It is both inward and outward reserve. The restraint of one's thoughts and feelings as well as of one's words and actions. Behaviors including self-control are learned responses. In other words, a person can develop self-control. That should be encouraging to you. But it also carries with it great responsibility. An individual with little self-control has only self to blame.

I heard a story recently about a man who went shopping with his wife and small child. He was taking care of the baby while his wife made a purchase. When the baby began to scream, the man quietly and repeatedly said, "Easy now, Albert, control your temper." A woman passing by complimented the dad and how he calmed his child. "Child nothing!" he replied. "My name is Albert, and I am just trying to control myself." Like the frustrated dad, we all need to learn self-discipline.

The world is out of control because of people who are undisciplined. Many illnesses and inappropriate behaviors are due to lack of control. In fact, many mental health experts believe that poor impulse control is at the root of many mental health disorders in the twenty-first century. It is apparent that individuals must learn personal discipline to prevent dysfunction and promote acceptable behavior.

Before moving to another perspective on "self-control," let's identify a few common synonyms for the noun _self-control_. Self-discipline, self-restraint, and reserve are words used to describe self-control. A popular synonym for self-control is "willpower." People talk openly about willpower—their own control of urges or actions. It is easy to bemoan poor willpower while enjoying a second helping of food or watching television instead of ironing clothes. The term *discipline* or *self-discipline* is generally defined as the training or conditions that develop improvement in physical or mental powers. Therefore, self-discipline leads to self-control. However, these terms are most often used interchangeably to mean personal restraint or willpower. Now let's see what the Bible has to say about the subject.

A Biblical Perspective

For the Christian, a better understanding of self-control comes only after careful study of Scripture. Both the Old and New Testaments address the topic of self-control. While the actual word *self-control* is not used in most translations of the Old Testament, its characteristics are described. The psalmist spoke of self-control. He encouraged the discipline of words and feelings in Psalm 19:14: *"May the words of my mouth and the meditation of my heart be acceptable to You, LORD, my rock and my Redeemer."* The Book of Proverbs discusses the impact of self-control: *"A man who does not control his temper is like a city whose wall is broken down"* (Proverbs 25:28).

Daniel is a positive example of self-control in the Old Testament. When he was invited to partake of the king's food and wine, he declined. Daniel 1:8 says that *"Daniel determined that he would not defile himself with the king's food or with the wine he drank. So he asked permission from the chief official not to defile himself."* The prophet resolved not to eat non-Kosher foods or drink wine served as offerings to Babylonian gods. His self-discipline strengthened Daniel for the work God had prepared for him.

The New Testament contains numerous passages with the word translated as self-control. Acts 24:25 is the first verse to mention self-control in the New Testament. Paul defended his faith to Felix, the governor of Judea, who had married Drusilla, the youngest daughter of Herod Agrippa I. In an undisciplined culture, the leader himself lacked personal discipline. Paul spoke boldly to Felix, whose morals were publically questioned, about *"righteousness, self-control, and the judgment to come"* (Acts 24:25). Felix became afraid and sent Paul away. The apostle's self-discipline was used by the Lord to accomplish His will.

The frequently used Greek word *egkrateia* means "the virtue of one who masters his desires and passions, especially his sensual appetites" (*Thayer's Greek-English Lexicon of the New Testament*). In Galatians 5:23, 1 Corinthians 9:25, 1 Timothy 3:2, and Titus 1:8, *egkrateia* is translated "self-control." It is described as a virtue of Christian living essential for spiritual maturity. Self-control, a fruit of the Holy Spirit, is not possible when a life is controlled by sin. Sin is a transgression against God, and therefore, the antithesis of self-control.

Spend some time now researching the biblical perspective of self-control. Find Scriptures including the word self-control listed in your concordance. Look up a definition of *self-control* in a Bible dictionary. Then, read the background on a Scripture passage about self-control from a commentary. **Record your findings below as an important discipline of personal Bible study.**

Concordance

_____

_____

Bible Dictionary

_____

_____

Commentary

_____

_____

By now, you have a better biblical understanding of self-control. Let's focus on a key Scripture passage. In his letter to the Galatian church, Paul described the fruit of the Spirit as *"love, joy, peace, patience, kindness, goodness, faith, gentleness, and self-control."* For Paul, self-control was not the last or the least of these virtues. In fact, self-control is the crowning fruit of the Spirit or the virtue necessary for all other virtues. Without self-control, a believer will not experience love, joy, peace, or any other blessing of the Spirit.

Paul emphasized the importance of self-control in several of his letters. In the first two chapters of the Book of Titus, Paul mentioned self-control at least five times. Dallas Willard talks about Paul's focus on self-control in his book, *The Spirit of the Disciplines*. Willard says of Paul's commitment that discipline was a "constant drumbeat in his life and writings." Self-control was obviously a virtue of Paul's life, enabling him to be productive for the Lord. Christians today must develop that same personal discipline in order to accomplish great work for the kingdom.

Many theologians have studied the concept of self-control. Commentaries on the New Testament Book of Galatians and books about the fruit of the Spirit add insights to the biblical perspective on self-control. In his commentary on Galatians, William Hendriksen explained that "self-control is the power to keep oneself in check." In his book, *The Spirit Within You*, Terry Young concluded that "self-control is the expression of the mature life which has learned to walk with God in perfect obedience." And pastor Jerry Bridges described self-control as "the believer's wall of defense against his inner man." Christians must build up the walls of defense around their lives through the practice of self-control.

Matthew Henry's commentary on Galatians compares and contrasts the deeds of the flesh and the fruit of the Spirit. Without self-control, a believer cannot resist the deeds of the flesh such as sexual immorality, idolatry, hatred, jealousy, dissension, drunkenness, orgies, and the like (Galatians 5:19–21). Without self-control, a believer cannot achieve the fruit of the Spirit including love, joy, peace, patience, kindness, goodness, faith, gentleness, and self-control (Galatians 5:22–23). It is not enough to cease to do evil. The believer must also learn to do good. "Our Christianity obliges us not only to die unto sin, but to live unto righteousness; not only to oppose the works of the flesh, but to bring forth the fruit of the Spirit" (*Matthew Henry Commentary*). Self-control does not simply say no to sin; it also says yes to godliness.

Jesus is the perfect example of a disciplined life. He not only resisted temptation but He lived for godliness. Because He was both man and God, Jesus fought the battle within Himself. While

His flesh was prone to sin, His Spirit was perfect in righteousness. **Read about the self-control of Jesus in His encounter with Pilate in Matthew 27:11–14. Explain how Jesus demonstrated self-control even as He faced His accusers.**

_____

_____

Though He was accused unjustly, Jesus remained silent before Pilate. When others testified against Him, Jesus didn't respond. A refusal to offer a defense was by Roman law an admission of guilt. However, Jesus disciplined Himself to not speak out and let God's will be accomplished.

There will be times in your life when you must exert self-control to resist sin or engage in godliness. Therefore, you must diligently seek to develop divine discipline more than human discipline. Your self-control is a reflection of a close personal relationship with the Holy Spirit. Self-control is clearly defined by authorities and carefully explained in Scripture. It also must be understood personally.

A Personal Reflection

Self-control must be personalized in order to be lasting. Not only must Christians learn what it is and how to develop it, but self-control must be applied individually to each believer's life. The process of application begins with conviction—an honest understanding that God wants to change your life.

The lesson of self-control has made a profound impact on my life personally. When God convicted me of my lack of discipline, I was shocked. From all outward appearances, I was a disciplined, productive individual. But God knew me well. He knew the areas of my life that were totally out of control. I was disciplined in several areas of my life and had been successful in disguising my undisciplined areas from others. But God knew my weaknesses and my excesses. He knew I hadn't turned my entire life over to Him. So I confessed my sin and acknowledged my lack of discipline.

Acknowledgment of your own lack of discipline is the first step in your journey toward self-control. So before going any further, do some soul-searching, some honest self-evaluation. **Are you practicing self-control in all areas of your life? Honestly answer yes or no, then explain.**

_____

_____

Once you have recognized your shortcomings and confessed them to the Lord, He promises to forgive them and restore you. Joyfully accept that promise of God written in 1 John 1:9: *"If we confess our sins, He is faithful and righteous to forgive us our sins and to cleanse us from all unrighteousness."* Then determine to be disciplined with the help of the Holy Spirit. But remember, recommitment to divine discipline is an ongoing process, a daily decision.

After I confessed my lack of discipline to the Lord and received His forgiveness, I determined to live a disciplined, righteous life. God personalized discipline in my life. First, He helped me see the need for physical discipline. I had let my body get out of control. Not only had I gained weight, but I was not living a healthy lifestyle. I was not exercising regularly or eating nutritiously. While it is very easy to overeat when you live in New Orleans (the food capital of the world!), I had let my eating get out of control. And I confess that physical discipline is an ongoing struggle for me personally. Life is busy, so there is little time for exercise. Food is delicious, and I have little willpower to resist. But self-control (even in eating) is the crowning fruit of the Spirit. So I must continue to practice restraint in my eating and determination in my exercise.

God has also convicted me personally about a lack of spiritual discipline. While I desire to grow in my faith and walk in the Spirit, I don't always do it. I start a Bible study but often don't finish. I begin to pray but get distracted. I desire to witness but I let fear grip me. I want to serve the Lord but I am busy doing my own thing, even though I want to be obedient to Him. To grow spiritually, I must discipline myself to do it! I must join a Bible study group that will hold me accountable. I must schedule my prayertime and stick with the schedule. I must identify an unsaved friend and boldly witness to her. I must volunteer to serve and do it to the best of my ability. I must practice spiritual discipline.

What about you? Do you understand what self-control is? Are you practicing self-control in your life? Or do you feel inadequate to be disciplined? Answer these questions in the space provided below.

_____

_____

_____

_____

A Christian life coach said self-discipline is one of the most common topics of discussion with his clients. He has concluded that one reason they fail to be disciplined is they believe they will eventually enjoy the undisciplined areas of their lives. Not true! He stresses the truth that "self-discipline is doing something even if you hate it or don't feel like doing it." In other words, discipline is not needed to do things you like. It is necessary to do the difficult things in life. You must discipline yourself to do those things difficult for you!

The Bible teaches that the believer has the Holy Spirit's presence and power to be disciplined. So there is hope for you and me. While we alone are unable to develop sufficient control of our desires and actions, God can help us be disciplined. Where your limited human willpower fails, God's supernatural power succeeds! Therefore, the Christian should practice personal willpower plus supernatural Godpower—or **divine discipline.** The power is from God, not from self.

Paul said it clearly in Titus 2:11–14 when he challenged Christians to accept the grace of God for salvation and godly living.

For the grace of God has appeared, with salvation for all people, instructing us to deny godlessness and worldly lusts and to live in a sensible, righteous, and godly way in the present age, while we wait *for the blessed hope and the appearing of the glory of our great God and Savior, Jesus Christ. He gave Himself for us to redeem us from all lawlessness and to cleanse for Himself a special people, eager to do good works. — Titus 2:11–14*

Divine discipline is Spirit-controlled discipline of oneself! It is not an innate behavior with which we are born—it is a learned behavior God wants to teach us. God is teaching me His divine discipline, and He wants to teach it to you! You must understand what it is, then receive His power to develop discipline in every area of your life.

My Personal Discipline

In this lesson, you have examined the meaning of *self-control*. You have learned that the believer has the power of God added to her own willpower—divine discipline. Explain what divine discipline means to you personally.

_____

_____

_____

Dear Lord:
Clarify the meaning of self-control in our minds so we can apply it in our lives. Amen.

Lesson 3
Outward Offenses and Discipline

Divine Instruction
Now the works of the flesh are obvious...as I told you before —
that those who practice such things will not inherit the kingdom of God
—Galatians 5:19–21

Now that we have examined the meaning of self-control, it is time to identify specific behaviors. Oh no, you may think. That is getting personal—it's meddling. But you cannot develop divine discipline until you understand the specific areas of your life that need to change. While you may feel that too many areas of your life are out of control, don't be overwhelmed. Let God reveal to you your weaknesses so that you can experience His strength. Once you identify your undisciplined behaviors, He will empower you to change.

The Bible speaks clearly about sin—rebellion against God. Sin results from an undisciplined life and can be expressed through ungodly outward behaviors or ungodly inward behaviors. This lesson will focus on outward behaviors that must be disciplined—words, deeds, and actions. Without discipline of your outward behaviors, you will not enjoy the fruit of the Spirit or experience spiritual growth.

As we look around the world we see evidence of uncontrolled outward behaviors.

- violence
- dishonesty
- lying
- stealing
- murder
- anger
- gossip
- overeating
- financial debt
- abuse

These are all evidences of lives without control. Everything that we say and do must be controlled by the Spirit. But often we allow our words and deeds to discourage rather than encourage. Undisciplined behaviors hurt others and harm our relationship with the Lord. Lack of self-control also hinders our witness. Scripture teaches us to control our outward behavior so we can be holy vessels, equipped to do God's work (2 Timothy 2:21).

Read 2 Timothy 2:20–21.
What does Paul teach about outward behavior in this passage?

_____

_____

_____

Believers are useful for the Master and prepared for every good work only when they are living godly lives. Sin diminishes our usefulness. Only when sinful behaviors are confessed can Jesus forgive and restore. Don't let sinful outward behaviors tarnish your witness or hinder your ministry.

In this lesson, we will examine ungodly behaviors to be avoided and godly behaviors to be practiced. The Bible clearly says no to sinfulness and yes to righteousness. While discipline is needed to resist temptation, discipline is also needed for faithfulness. The faith in our hearts must be consistently lived out in our lives. It is essential for believers walking in the Spirit to avoid unrighteousness, engage in holiness, and purpose to do godliness.

Avoid Unrighteousness

Just before the Apostle Paul discussed the fruit of the Spirit in Galatians 5:22–23, he warned about the deeds of the flesh. He understood our sinful natures and knew that discipline was needed to overcome our own evil desires. We are definitely born with a sinful nature. The Scripture says, *"all have sinned and fall short of the glory of God"* (Romans 3:23). We see that sinful nature frequently in a young child who must be taught right from wrong. A two-year-old child not only does what is wrong, but a two-year old wants to make sure the misconduct is seen by everyone. That child must be disciplined and be taught self-discipline.

Read Galatians 5:19-21 to see some of the outward behaviors that must be disciplined. List those deeds of the flesh below.

1. _____   6. _____   11. _____

2. _____   7. _____   12. _____

3. _____   8. _____   13. _____

4. _____   9. _____   14. _____

5. _____   10. _____   15. _____

What do you think Paul meant by *"and anything similar"* **in verse 21?**

_____

_____

Were you surprised by the long list of deeds of the flesh when Paul only cites nine fruit of the Spirit in Galatians 5:22–23? This list of ungodly behaviors is evidence of the sinful human nature of man. And the list goes on; it is even longer than the list given in Scripture. Paul implied that with "and anything similar"—in other words, etc., etc., etc.

God knew that Adam and Eve would sin in the Garden of Eden. He warned them not to eat of the tree of knowledge of good and evil though He knew that they would deliberately disobey Him (Genesis 3:17). God knows that we will sin today because we are human and have a sinful nature. God reminds us of our deeds of the flesh so that we can be disciplined to walk in the Spirit. Though our society accepts certain uncontrolled behavior and encourages other unacceptable actions, Christians are to avoid unrighteousness in obedience to God's law.

Paul, in his writings to the Christian church, gave much attention to the sins of the flesh. In fact, he included a plea for purity in each of his letters. The list in Galatians 5 actually addresses the sins of the flesh in relationship to God, man, and self, just as Paul relates the fruit of the Spirit. The sins against God include heresy, idolatry, sorcery, worshiping other gods or other spirits, and accepting opinions contrary to God's Word (Galatians 5:20). The sins against man include hatred, strife, jealousy, anger, selfish ambition, dissension, envy, and murder (Galatians 5:20–21). The sins against self include substance abuse and sexual immorality (Galatians 5:21). God teaches His children to abstain from evil doings—to avoid unrighteousness.

There are many evidences today of poor self-control in outward behavior. Gail MacDonald mentions six symptoms of what she calls "the unsharpened life" in her book, *Keep Climbing*: poor mouth control, ungodly peer standards, excessive whininess or self-pity, over-investment in tasks and short-changed relationships, inner deceit, and disobedience to the laws of God. Did Gail MacDonald step on your toes with this contemporary list of sinful behaviors? Ouch! She surely did step on mine.

Take a few minutes to consider this list of unrighteous behaviors. Do you have any outward behaviors that are harming your relationship with God, others, or yourself? If so, list them below.

Sinfulness toward God_____

_____

_____

Sinfulness toward others _____

_____

_____

Sinfulness toward self _____

_____

_____

These ungodly behaviors hurt you—your relationship toward God, other people, and yourself. Self-discipline is needed for godliness.

As I reread Gail MacDonald's list of ungodly behaviors, I was convicted. I must confess that I often have poor mouth control. Since I love to talk, I have many opportunities to speak unkind words. Though I don't mean to harm others with critical comments, harsh words seem to come out of my uncontrolled mouth. Though my intentions may have been humorous, my remarks may hurt the receiver. *Lord, tame my tongue! Help me control my mouth so I speak only words that help, not hurt. Let every word I speak be pleasing to You and encouraging to others. Amen.*

If you also have an untamed tongue, I suggest that you read Ephesians 4:25–32 and James 3:5–12. They remind us to speak the truth in love and to avoid negative, critical speech. Only God can tame an uncontrolled tongue. These passages of Scripture and many more reinforce the need for discipline of outward behaviors.

A blatant example of uncontrolled, unsportsman-like behavior was captured on television during a recent football game. A player of the winning team ran along the sideline near the opposing team's side. Suddenly a coach deliberately tripped the player. As he fell to the ground, everyone in the stadium gasped. The team was penalized and the coach was fined. Though many of the players along the sidelines may have thought about tripping the opponent, they didn't. They controlled themselves. In a follow-up interview, the coach apologized for his lack of control. Discipline of outward behavior is always needed.

Self-control is necessary in our relationship with God, others, and self. Discipline of outward behavior pleases God, encourages others, and strengthens self. Discipline of outward behavior is only possible if you avoid unrighteousness and engage in holiness.

Engage in Holiness

During my teenage years, my Christian parents often warned me to avoid unrighteousness. But they also encouraged me to engage in holiness. In fact, my dad often said, "If you are busy doing good things for God, you won't have time to do bad things with the devil." How true! My parents kept me busy with church activities and Christian friends as they prayed that I would stay close to the

Lord. Today I remain active in my church and close to my Christian friends. I also discipline myself to grow in the Lord and live a godly life. Spiritual discipline takes time!

A disciplined Christian makes time for God. No matter how busy or how mature, a growing believer spends time daily with the Lord. Disciplined daily devotions promote self-control in outward behaviors and inward desires. Conversely, inconsistent quiet times open the door for disobedience and misbehavior. A believer can be protected from unrighteousness by engaging in holiness.

Spiritual discipline is essential in the areas of prayer, Bible study, witness, and service. It is important to be involved in public worship and praise in addition to personal prayer and study. All followers of Christ are commanded to grow in their faith through daily spiritual disciplines. Faith falters when faith isn't flourishing!

Read the following Scriptures and note how the Bible teaches all believers to engage in holiness.

1 John 5:14–15 _____

_____

2 Timothy 2:15 _____

_____

Colossians 4:2–6 _____

_____

Mark 10:43–45 _____

_____

Every Christian is to be disciplined in spiritual life and outward behaviors. Prayer is essential for the believer to know God's will and to learn how to live a godly life (1 John 5:14–15). Bible study is necessary to know the truth and understand how to live it

(2 Timothy 2:15). Witnessing is the natural expression of a believer who loves the Lord and wants to share Him with others (Colossians 4:2–6). Service, though time consuming, ministers to others and models godliness after Christ Himself (Mark 10:43–45). These spiritual disciplines are essential to Christian growth.

In what areas are you undisciplined spiritually? You must identify your own weaknesses in order to grow stronger. Dallas Willard, in *The Spirit of the Disciplines*, says, "The need for extensive practice of a given discipline is an indication of our weakness, not our strength. We can even lay it down as a rule of thumb that if it is easy for us to engage in a certain discipline, we don't need to practice it." **What spiritual discipline is the most difficult for you to practice regularly? Why?**

_____

_____

_____

God may want you to focus on that area of your spiritual life and develop divine discipline.

God often reminds me of my need to witness. Sharing my faith with others doesn't come to me easily or naturally. It should, but it doesn't. I grew up as the daughter of an evangelist. His bold testimony was so powerful, it made my witness seem weak. I married an evangelism professor. His depth of knowledge made my witnessing seem shallow. But God challenges me to find my own way to witness of Him. I must be disciplined to speak a good word about Jesus and talk about what He is doing in my life. When I practice this spiritual discipline, I am engaging in holiness and I can be used by Him.

Just recently I asked the Lord to give me an opportunity to be a witness of him on a flight. I prayed for boldness and an opportunity to start the conversation. God answered my prayer as I was settling into my seat. The pleasant man next to me asked about my work. As I began telling him about my ministry, he confessed to being a Christian not living for the Lord. We talked about the importance of prayer, Bible study, and church involvement. I made some suggestions and offered to pray for him. I trust God is at work in His life now. God honored my decision to be a witness.

With God's help, we can discipline our outward behaviors. He wants to help us avoid unrighteousness and engage in holiness. He wants to give us His strength to overcome our weakness. He can and He will if we practice spiritual discipline and purpose for godliness.

Purpose for Godliness

A disciplined lifestyle demands daily self-control. Outward behaviors will become destructive without control and will flounder without direction. Direction or purpose is essential to a productive life. Every individual needs to develop a definite purpose in life. The believer must purpose for godliness—be determined to live a life committed to God.

What is your purpose in life? What goal is the focus of all your effort? It is helpful to consider what you hope to accomplish with your life. **If you have never done it before, take time to develop a purpose statement for your life. Write your personal purpose statement here.**

_____

_____

_____

A person's purpose statement should guide the activities of life. Without a purpose or direction, a person works a lot but accomplishes nothing. With a clear purpose, a person can achieve many goals. While daily activities may change, a life purpose should never change. For the Christian, the primary life purpose should be to know and do the will of God. Every believer should purpose for godliness. Divine discipline is needed to focus on that purpose and keep it central to all activities.

Read Philippians 3:13–14 to learn about Paul's personal purpose statement. Fill in the blanks below to complete the Scripture.

Brothers, I do not consider myself to have taken hold of it. But _____ thing I do: forgetting what is _____ _____ and reaching _____ to what is ahead, I pursue as my _____ the _____ promised by God's heavenly _____ in Christ Jesus.

The Apostle Paul was a man with a single purpose. His only focus in life was to know God. He accomplished many things—he wrote half of the New Testament and started churches all over the Roman world. He was busy doing the work of the Lord, but Paul steadfastly maintained his single purpose. Like Paul, believers today must have a central focus—to know God. If we discipline ourselves to know Him, we will receive the prize—His prize. Our purpose is discipline; our prize is heaven.

At the beginning of each new year, I review my personal achievements and reaffirm my life purpose. I actually make a list of long-term and short-term goals in specific areas of my life—spiritual, physical, mental, and social. But my list is meaningless without a purpose statement. Several years ago I developed a purpose statement to guide my life activities. It is based on Philippians 3:13–14. Though it took me numerous attempts, I settled on the following statement: "With God's help, I will continue to grow spiritually and personally as I minister and witness in His power." Daily discipline is necessary for my purpose for godliness. You must also commit daily to purpose for godliness and discipline your outward behaviors.

In his book, *Celebration of Discipline*, Richard Foster gives principles for controlling outward behavior. His advice can help us avoid unrighteousness, engage in holiness, and purpose for godliness:

- Buy things for their usefulness rather than their status. If you need it, buy it.
- Don't buy it because it looks good to others.
- Reject anything that is producing an addiction in you. Limit yourself in activities or practices that can become habit-forming.
- Develop a habit of giving things away. When you have no further use for something, give it away or share it with another.

- Refuse to be propagandized by the custodians of modern gadgetry. Timesaving devices usually cost more but rarely save time. Invest in original, do-it-yourself models.
- Learn to enjoy things without owning them. Many things in life can be enjoyed without owning them if we control our spending.
- Develop a deeper appreciation for the creation. Enjoy God's beautiful world as you control your excesses.
- Look with a healthy skepticism at all "buy now, pay later" schemes. Don't allow yourself to become in debt and under the control of others.
- Obey Jesus' instructions about plain, honest speech. Be truthful and dependable in your communication with others.
- Reject anything that breeds the oppression of others. Don't exploit others through your own selfish ambitions.
- Shun anything that distracts you from seeking first the kingdom of God. Try to focus on your spiritual journey.

These practical guidelines will help you discipline your outward behaviors and develop a godly lifestyle. It will not be an easy task, but for the believer, God promises help. With His divine discipline, you can live a godly life.

As I reread those suggestions, I was convicted by a couple of them. It is Christmas time so expenses are high. I have renewed a personal commitment to control my spending. I will pay cash and not charge purchases so we will not accrue debt. And, we have determined to give gifts with a purpose. I purchased many Christmas gifts this year from the craft fair that was held at the seminary—we got presents to give to others and helped out the students who were selling the items. We bought many gifts through our church to support ministries in our community, in our country, and around the world. Discipline yourself in your outward behavior and be a blessing to others.

Read 2 Timothy 2:20–21 again. What is the promise to those who discipline their outward behaviors? Complete this sentence, "If anyone purifies himself, he will be..."

_____

_____

What a precious promise! As we discipline our outward behaviors we become a vessel for honor, righteous in behavior, useful to the Master—prepared for every good work.

Discipline of outward behavior is necessary for the believer's relationship with God and ministry to others. It is also imperative to discipline inward behaviors—thoughts, feelings, and emotions. As the Bible says, *"Guard your heart above all else, for it is the source of life"* (Proverbs 4:23). In the next lesson, we will examine our inward instincts. Discipline of both your lifestyle and your heart is needed for spiritual growth!

My Personal Discipline

With the guidance of the Holy Spirit, make a plan to engage in holiness in the following areas. Write down your plan and begin today.

Bible Study _____

_____

Prayer _____

_____

Witnessing _____

_____

Service _____

_____

Dear Lord:
Give me the power to control my outward behaviors so I will avoid unrighteousness, engage in holiness, and purpose for godliness all the days of my life. Amen.

Lesson 4
Inward Instincts and Discipline

Divine Instruction

Guard your heart above all else, for it is the source of life. — Proverbs 4:23

A Christian's greatest challenge today is living a life not conformed to the world. To be in the world but not of the world is the Bible's command (Romans 12:2). Personal discipline is necessary if biblical guidelines are to be applied to lifestyles. Outward behaviors must be controlled because they reflect the inward spirit. The inner being influences outward actions. So both outward behaviors and inward instincts must be disciplined. Body and soul—actions and attitudes—need restraint.

In my own personal pilgrimage I have found it easier to control my outward behaviors than my thoughts, desires, and feelings. My mother carefully taught me the discipline of what I say and do. I must confess that I sometimes struggle in doing that! But I also learned that no one can control my thoughts but me. While I may inhibit what I say, I can still have bad thoughts. I may not say, "I really don't like you," but I often think that—and more. While I do not hurt people with unacceptable actions, I do sometimes hope that cruel things happen to them. My uncontrolled thoughts and feelings can run rampant!

Do you have trouble controlling your inward behaviors? What unkind feelings do you harbor toward others? What ungodly thoughts cloud your mind? What selfish passions motivate your actions? **Record here any uncontrolled inner instincts. As you write them, ask God to transform your heart.**

The Bible teaches that true beauty is more than skin deep. Outward appearance is reflective of the heart. The countenance of a beautiful woman is an expression of the condition of her spirit. Beauty is more than an attractive face or stylish fashions. True beauty comes from within and is evidenced by a love for God and concern for others. No amount of makeup or even expensive clothes can cover up a selfish heart, unkind words, or hurtful actions.

Proverbs 4:23 says: *"Guard your heart above all else, for it is the source of life."* Your life literally flows out of your heart. It is clear that a Christian must discipline her inward instincts as well as her outward behaviors. You must develop and maintain control of your passion for possessions, your feelings toward your fellowman, and your Christian character. Then you will enjoy the abundant life in Him.

Passion for Possessions

What are the passions of your heart? *Merriam-Webster's* dictionary says *passion* is "an intense, driving, overmastering feeling or conviction." The passions of our hearts are often physical desires, sexual fantasies, or material obsessions. These natural passions are temporal; they give only momentary pleasure. But they are typical of our sinful human natures.

For a few minutes, focus on your own uncontrolled passions. What intense feelings, drives, or convictions do you have? They may be material possessions, selfish ideas, or self-gratifying experiences that you feel about strongly. List them here.

_____

_____

While I do have too many selfish passions, shopping may be the one I practice most often. My husband says I have three spiritual gifts not mentioned in the Bible—shopping, sleeping, and talking. Well, he's right. I love to shop, sleep, and talk—and I am good at all three endeavors. In fact, I am passionate about them. Shopping brings me great joy and helps me relax. But because I also love clothes, shopping can be a problem for me. Though I have a specific clothing budget, it is insufficient to fulfill my *desire* for clothes. I must discipline myself while shopping. Sometimes I must leave my purse, including my credit cards, at home when I go out shopping. Most often, I must shop with a list and only buy what is on the list. Even though my actions may be controlled, I still have a heartfelt passion for those material possessions.

Christians are commanded to discipline their desires — to flee their flesh — to control their carnal natures — to purify their passions. God empowers believers to do that with His divine discipline. David, king of Israel, struggled with his own uncontrolled nature. He acknowledged the importance of inward discipline in Psalm 19:14: *"May the words of my mouth and the meditation of my heart be acceptable to You, LORD, my rock and my Redeemer."* **What does that verse mean to you? Rewrite its meaning in your own words.**

_____

_____

While others know only our outward behaviors, our hearts are known only to God. He knows our thoughts, our desires, and our feelings. And He wants the "meditations of our hearts" to be pleasing to Him — to be godly. That is possible through the power of God and His redeeming love.

The Apostle Paul discussed the consequences of an ungodly heart in his letter to the Christians in Rome. **Read Romans 1:18–32 to learn of God's wrath on unrighteousness. How does God respond to our ungodly behavior? Summarize His response in the space provided below.**

_____

_____

Lusts and passions of the heart lead to sinful behavior and judgment by God. Because He is a just and loving God, He promises to forgive sin and empower us for godly living. Satan, however, wants our uncontrolled passions to destroy us.

Gordon MacDonald wrote candidly about the deceit of the devil in his book, *Rebuilding Your Broken World*. He said, "There came a time when dragons, if you please, had come through my gates and had caught hold of my mind and my choice-making mechanisms." All of us are susceptible to sin because of our carnal natures. Ungodly passions and desires often sneak in by night, catching us off guard. God's people must control their passions.

When my dad left the ministry and our family, he turned his back on the Lord. We are grateful to say that he has returned to the Lord and renewed his relationship with us. Dad has often shared his testimony of restoration with others. Though immorality and unfaithfulness were his visible sins, he is quick to concede that his ungodly passions began in his heart. He encourages others to passionately seek the Lord and the truth of His Word — to guard their hearts as well as their lives.

John Bunyan, author of *The Pilgrim's Progress*, a literary classic, confessed that his sin was a natural result of his wicked heart:

> Sin and corruption would bubble up out of my heart as naturally as water bubbles up from a fountain. I thought now that everyone had a better heart than I had. I could have changed hearts with anybody. I thought none but the devil himself could equalize me for inward wickedness and pollution of mind. I fell, therefore, at the sight of my own vileness, deeply into despair, for I concluded that this condition in which I was in could not stand with a life of grace. Sure, thought I, I am forsaken of God; sure I am given up to the devil and to a reprobate mind.

As did John Bunyan, we must realize that we have evil hearts. Our inward wickedness is a fact. But we are not forsaken by God. He gives us the power to control the wickedness of our hearts. God helps us overcome our sinful natures. Our responsibility is to "take heed," "set a watch," and "be vigilant" to discipline the passions of our hearts.

The desires of our hearts can quickly become a passion for possessions or a lust for love if we do not resist evil. God's warning is clear — "abstain from evil." He doesn't just say "be careful" or "pray about it." He says, "abstain!" That means have nothing to do with evil; flee from sin. We must use self-control to resist the temptation of the devil. Remember, the devil is like a roaring lion seeking whom he may devour (1 Peter 5:8). He will destroy you if you let your guard down, if you don't discipline your inward instincts.

God will help you have a disciplined heart; He will help you control your passions and desires. He will also empower you to control your feelings for your fellowman and be concerned for your own character.

Feelings for Fellowman

Some people are easy to love; others are much more difficult to love. But the Bible says we are to love everyone, for love is of God (1 John 4:7–11). If God loves us, we ought to love one another. God gives us that type of unconditional love. And He will help us have unconditional love, controlling our thoughts and feelings about others. Our feelings toward our spouse, our children, our families, and our friends can become unkind and unloving. We may be irritated by their actions and hurt by their criticisms. It takes self-control to love people, even those closest to you. God can help you discipline your feelings for your fellowman.

How do you feel about your fellowman? Take a few minutes to analyze your true feelings about those closest to you. Write in the space below your honest evaluation about your feelings toward:

Your spouse _____

_____

Your children_____

_____

Your family _____

_____

Your friends_____

_____

Remember what the Bible says about feelings toward others: *"And be kind and compassionate to one another, forgiving one another, just as God also forgave you in Christ"* (Ephesians 4:32). You must discipline your feelings of frustration and anger. You must develop an attitude of love and kindness. You must forgive others of even their most painful sin against you. You must forgive others because God has so graciously forgiven you.

The Lord wants to help you control your feelings about others. In fact, immediately prior to His command in Ephesians 4:32, the Bible tells us what grieves the Holy Spirit. **Read Ephesians 4:31–32, and identify five ungodly behaviors that grieve the Holy Spirit in verse 31. Write them below.**

1. _____

2. _____

3. _____

4. _____

5. _____

Bitterness, wrath, anger, tensions, and unwholesome words grieve the Lord (Ephesians 4:31). Those unrighteous feelings break the heart of God and must be eliminated from the Christian's life. God can help us control those feelings. He can help us see good in everyone, though we must look carefully and be determined. As we practice divine discipline, we can replace those ungodly feelings toward others with love, kindness, and encouragement. But it takes self-control to show kindness in this unkind world.

My sister Mitzi believes in speaking her mind. We tease her that she needs a filter to keep her thoughts from coming out of her mouth. What she thinks, she says. When her comments seem harsh, she likes to say, "But they're true." Well, sometimes they are. But, Christians must control their speech and always speak the truth in love. It is important for us to discipline our feelings for our fellow-man and love them in the name of Jesus.

In her book, *Don't Miss the Blessing*, JoAnn Leavell challenges readers to love one another, to be kind to each other. She suggests that we (1) affirm others, (2) encourage them, and (3) minister to them. She says, "A proven way to help yourself is by helping other people, because when you seek happiness for others, you find it for yourself." That is the reward of self-control! The discipline needed to love others pays off in the end. You will be blessed as you bless those around you!

Loving feelings for others are an overflow of a heart committed to Jesus. As our hearts overflow with God's grace and glory, we feel love and mercy toward our fellowman. We must discipline our feelings if we are serious about our relationships with the Lord. Negative thoughts must be eliminated and positive feelings must be established. Your thoughts about others reflect your thoughts about God. The disciplined heart results in controlled passions and feelings. The disciplined heart also demonstrates a concern for personal character.

Concern for Character

Society today accepts an inaccurate assumption—the idea that the character of a person doesn't matter. But character does matter! The Bible teaches that who you are, the person you are, is just as important as what you say or do. While the world believes that your personal problems don't matter if you are doing your job well, the Bible says the heart and life cannot be separated. Christians must be concerned about character—their inner selves.

While the Bible records the many mighty works of God, it also proclaims the character of God. God's character is clearly described in Scripture. **What are the attributes of God's character that mean a lot to you? List below some descriptors of God. He is**

_____

_____

Among His many attributes, the Bible says that God is:

Good — Psalm 34:8
Holy — Isaiah 6:3
Loving — 1 John 4:8–10
Merciful — Psalm 118
Patient — Numbers 14:18
Personal — Exodus 33:14
Sovereign — Colossians 1:15–18

Because He is God and His character is perfect, all positive traits can be attributed to Him. Biblical instruction for praise includes gratitude to God for who He is as well as for what He has done (Psalm 150). If the character of God is important, the character of His children is important too.

It has been said that "character is what a person is in the dark." In other words, who you are is best seen in what you do when you think no one is looking. Your true nature is exposed in private. The better you know someone, the more you know her true character. Character, the inner person, must be controlled.

In Proverbs 10, the wise sayings of King Solomon are recorded. He contrasts wisdom and foolishness in a righteous and unrighteous man. Wisdom brings joy to a father, but foolishness grieves a mother (v. 1). Righteousness brings blessings, but unrighteousness results in violence (v. 6). He who walks in integrity is secure; he who perverts his ways is lost (v. 9). Clear contrasts between the righteous and the wicked continue in this proverb until Solomon concludes in verses 27 through 32. **Read Proverbs 10:27–32 then fill in the blanks below.**

The fear of the LORD prolongs life,
    but the years of the _____ *are cut short.*
The hope of the _____ *is joy,*
    but the expectation of the _____ *comes to nothing.*
The way of the LORD is a stronghold for the _____,
    but destruction awaits the _____.
The _____ *will never be shaken,*
    but the _____ *will not remain on the earth.*

The mouth of the _____ produces wisdom,
*   but a _____ tongue will be cut out.*
The lips of the _____ know what is appropriate,
*   but the mouth of the _____, only what is perverse.*

Character does matter to God. What a person is within will be reflected outwardly!

Wisdom and integrity are expressed in words of kindness and acts of love. Righteous behavior brings honor to God, while unrighteousness brings destruction. God wants to help you control your character so that your life will bring glory to Him and not destruction to yourself.

Character is simply "the complex of mental and ethical traits marking and often individualizing a person," according to *Merriam-Webster's* dictionary. Character is made up of attributes and qualities, which form personalities. Each person has a unique personality, an individual temperament. For every personality there are both strengths and weaknesses. Each personality must be controlled. In fact, strengths of a personality left uncontrolled can become weaknesses. Let's briefly examine the area of personalities to learn what the Lord wants to control.

There are several basic types of temperaments or personalities. The four-temperament theory, which originated with Hippocrates, continues to be the most widely accepted explanation of human behavior. Tim LaHaye wrote about these personalities in his book, *Spirit-Controlled Temperament*, and later in a sequel, *Your Temperament: Discover Its Potential*. He described the four basic categories as *sanguine, choleric, melancholy,* and *phlegmatic*. As his book title suggests, LaHaye wrote that the Holy Spirit can control the temperaments of believers.

The *sanguine* personality is generally warm, outgoing, happy, and fun-loving (the "popular" personality). The *choleric* is typically hot, strong-willed, self-sufficient, and very independent (the "powerful" personality). The *melancholy* is an analytical, self-sacrificing, perfectionistic type with a very sensitive emotional nature (the "perfect" personality). And the *phlegmatic* is the calm, easygoing individual who is a peacemaker (the "peaceful" personality). As you can imagine, most people are combinations of these four basic temperaments. And all temperaments have tendencies that must be controlled.

Have you begun to identify your own personality type? Have you recognized the strengths and weaknesses of your own temperament? Answer these questions.

What is your primary personality type? _____

_____

What are your personality strengths? _____

_____

_____

What are your personality weaknesses? _____

_____

_____

Understanding your own personality is important because only then can you discipline your weaknesses and develop your strengths. It is also helpful to understand the personalities of others. Then you can relate well to each other, and you can encourage each other to grow as you understand one another's character.

The body of Christ is a unique blend of personalities. Though all are created in the image of God, we have our own personalities. Christians often have difficulties getting along. We must learn to control some of the weaknesses of our character so that we can relate to each other in love. When character faults emerge, tensions rise. Christians must discipline themselves in all areas to function as the healthy body of Christ.

Florence Littauer also discussed temperaments in her book, *Personality Plus,* and in several other books. She summarized two reasons for studying the temperaments: "First, examine our own strengths and weaknesses, and learn how to accentuate our positives and eliminate our negatives; and second, understand other people, and realize that just because someone is different does not make him wrong." Christians must want to discipline their temperaments, to control their characters.

Outward behaviors and inward instincts need discipline because God cares about our lives and our hearts. As Christians grow spiritually, we receive God's gift of inner righteousness and godly character. But that spiritual growth requires discipline, resulting in Christlike actions and a pure heart. Pray today that God will teach you inner discipline, which will then produce outer godliness. Also ask the Lord to strengthen you step-by-step as you develop and maintain self-control.

My Personal Discipline

You have read Proverbs 4:23 as you studied this lesson. Now read the passage which contains the verse—Proverbs 4:20-27. Why is it so important for you to *"guard your heart above all else"*? **Summarize your response in the space below.**

_____

_____

Dear Lord:
Help me to accept myself as Your divine creation and to depend on Your power to control my passions, feeling, and character. Then You can truly produce the fruit of the Spirit in my life. Amen.

Lesson 5
My Own Willpower for Discipline

Divine Instruction
For God has not given us a spirit of fearfulness, but one of power, love, and sound judgment —2 Timothy 1:7

A t a craft fair, I saw a wooden wall plaque of a cute little pig. On it were painted the words, "I just ate my willpower." I don't know about you, but I have always believed that I have no willpower. I feel incapable of controlling my urges, especially my desire for food. That is why I identified with the fat pig. God has convinced me that I do have willpower—I must use it!

God created man and woman in His image, equal with worth and value (Genesis 1:27). God doesn't make any mistakes. If you believe that, then you must agree that you have personal willpower. God has given each of us the ability to control our own behaviors. Some of us are naturally more disciplined than others are, but all of God's children have willpower. He can help us develop and use it more fully in order to live a godly life.

On the scale below, honestly rate your personal willpower. Do you have little willpower (0 = none) or great willpower (10 = excellent)? Mark the number with an X.

0   1   2   3   4   5   6   7   8   9   10

No willpower   **Excellent willpower**

Your willpower may vary from day to day or minute to minute. Different types of activity may also affect your willpower. My willpower often wavers when I am tired or spiritually dry, or when I need to do something I do not enjoy. That is why we must be disciplined to stay close to the Lord and avoid inevitable temptations.

Willpower is defined in the Collins dictionary as "the ability to control oneself and determine one's actions." It is the firmness of mind. I understand willpower to be personal determination to "stick to" a task. When natural inclination is to quit, willpower encourages a person not to give up. God has given all of His children—the weak and the strong—an adequate supply of willpower. In addition, God empowers His children to be even stronger—to be disciplined.

In the Garden of Eden, Adam and Eve had willpower—they simply chose not to use it. Their lack of discipline hindered them personally and has impacted human beings throughout time. **Turn in your Bible to Genesis 3:1–19. Read the account of the sin of Adam and Eve. Try to understand their weak willpower as you answer the following questions:**

Why did Eve sin (see verse 6)? _____

_____

What was the penalty for her sin (see verse 16)? _____

_____

Why did Adam sin (see verse 6)? _____

_____

What was the penalty for his sin (see verses 17–19)? _____

_____

The snake didn't make Eve sin in the garden. He tempted her—the forbidden fruit was "good," "delightful," and "desirable" (Genesis 3:6). It was Eve who chose to disobey God. She didn't use her God-given willpower to resist the temptation and avoid the fruit. Adam could also have refused the fruit. They followed their own desires and brought sin into the world. Each of us sins when we don't use the willpower God has given us to resist temptation.

Self-discipline is the result of a conscious choice to do what ought to be done. Each person chooses to be controlled or uncontrolled in thinking and living. The first step in this process is the personal decision to be disciplined. No one—not even God—can make the decision to be disciplined for us.

In this chapter, we will analyze our own willpower. Prayerfully consider the personal commitment, the ideal conditions, and the lifestyle changes needed in your pursuit of self-control. Man is God's only creation given the power of choice. With that privilege comes great responsibility—we must make good choices. So we must make personal commitments to do right, to live godly lives. The first step toward divine discipline involves choice and commitment. Though commitment is not encouraged by the world, God requires it. Each of us must personally make a commitment to be disciplined. You must decide to do it!

Personal Commitment

The Bible teaches believers about the two ways—the choice to obey or disobey, the choice to sin or follow God. **Read the parable told by Jesus in Matthew 7:13–14. What happens to the many who follow their own ways? Answer that question based on Scripture in the space provided below.**

_____

_____

Destruction is the result of sin, rebellion against the will of God. Believers must be committed to God's way even when the world is following another path.

In his famous poem, "The Road Not Taken," Robert Frost concluded: "I took the road less traveled by, and that has made all the difference." Many factors influence the roads we travel. But the traveler ultimately must decide which road to follow. For the Christian, the disciplined, godly life is the road less traveled. Most people follow the undisciplined, ungodly life. You must choose! If you choose to follow God's way to godliness, that will make all the difference.

To be disciplined in life, you must make a commitment—you must decide to do it. First, you must decide personally. No one else can make this choice for you. It is your sole responsibility. Marjorie Holmes made a personal decision to be disciplined physically. In her book, *Secrets of Health, Energy, and Staying Young*, she relates the personal decision she made as a child: "All dad's people were on the fat side; mother's were lean. I decided to take after my mother's people. Deep in my soul I resolved never, never to be fat." Throughout her life, Marjorie Holmes has been slim and vivacious. Though genetics may have been working in her favor, she also made a personal commitment. She decided to do it! You will be faced with many decisions in your life. I encourage you to make the personal commitment to follow Christ and make the decision to pursue divine discipline.

Your decision must be personal, and it must be sincere. A decision to follow the Lord and be disciplined must be genuine. The decision cannot be artificial or contrived. It must be honest and from the heart or it won't last. The decision cannot be motivated by selfish gain but by sincere godliness. The believer must honestly desire to be like Christ and resist the temptations of the world.

Many Christians make a sincere, personal commitment when they are called to the full-time ministry. Discipline is needed as they follow God's will in their lives and callings. Often they pursue seminary training to equip themselves for more effective service. Seminary students must exercise great personal discipline to succeed at their school work while balancing the demands of family, work, and ministry. Their daily discipline is based on the personal commitments they have made to follow Christ and fulfill His calling.

A disciplined life requires good choices. You must decide sincerely, but you must also decide daily. The commitment to discipline is not a onetime decision. It is a daily recommitment to self-control with the help and the power of the Lord. Discipline will not last for a lifetime without a daily commitment. Like salvation, a commitment to the Lord must be renewed each and every day.

Identify the following statements below as true or false. Place a check mark beside your response, then briefly explain your answer.

I have decided *personally* to lead a disciplined life.

True ___ Why? _____

False ___ Why? _____

I have decided *sincerely* to lead a disciplined life.

True ___ Why? _____

False ___ Why? _____

I have decided *daily* to lead a disciplined life.

True ___ Why? _____

False ___ Why? _____

When I decided to develop discipline in my life, it was a decision I made personally, sincerely, and daily. It was October 12, 1987 (a Monday, of course), when I made the decision to do it! It was *my* decision. No one else could decide for me—not my loving husband or concerned mother. I decided to be disciplined. It was a sincere decision. More than ever before, I really wanted to get control of my life. I wanted God to help me be disciplined in all areas of my life. And that decision has been daily. As I face my personal weaknesses and the world's temptations, I must recommit myself every day to personal discipline. If my daily decision is forgotten, my discipline falters.

The first step toward self-discipline is a personal commitment—a deliberate decision to take action. You alone must take that step! Now that we've discussed the need for personal willpower, let's talk about the ideal conditions and the lifestyle changes necessary for disciplined Christian living.

While God has given us personal willpower to which He will add His supernatural power, He also calls on us to create an atmosphere that will encourage self-discipline. Discipline is definitely promoted in a controlled context. Jesus told us that *"The spirit is willing, but the flesh is weak"* (Matthew 26:41). **What does that Bible verse mean to you?**

_____

_____

Ideal Conditions

Jesus knew that even when our hearts desire godliness, it is difficult to resist temptation with our sinful natures in a sinful world. We must try to surround ourselves with positive influences. If we build an environment that encourages vigilance and restraint, we will find self-control easier to develop and maintain.

Paul gave instruction to his friend Timothy about the importance of surroundings. In 1 Timothy 6:11–12, Paul challenged Timothy to flee greed and pursue godliness, to fight temptation and seek eternal life. Foolish and harmful lusts certainly lead to destruction (1 Timothy 6:9). **Read 1 Timothy 6:11–12. Discuss what you understand God to desire for you in relationship to sin and virtue.**

_____

_____

Paul knew that young Timothy would have trouble leading a godly life in a world filled with corruption. He needed to run from evil and surround himself with good in order to live a blameless life. For new believers, this may mean limiting contact with old friends who are a bad influence or abandoning places that foster immorality. Every believer must try to avoid temptations in order to control inevitable vulnerabilities. While there are some circumstances in your life that you cannot bypass, there are many situations you can avoid!

I have a friend who was addicted to drugs for many years. When he came to know the Lord, he was able to conquer the control of those harmful substances. He is living for the Lord and serving Him daily. However, he faces strong temptation as he ministers to others with substance abuse. He has faltered twice, influenced by the environment in which he now works.

God's power has restored him as he disciplined himself to resist temptation. My prayer is that he will commit himself daily to the Lord. However, I wonder if he should delay his ministry in a drug center until his self-discipline is stronger.

Gordon MacDonald relates a counseling experience in his book, *Rebuilding Your Broken World*. A guilt-ridden Christian man became involved in a one-night affair while on a business trip. He was concerned about the impact of his infidelity on his marriage. MacDonald encouraged the remorseful man to think back on how he could have avoided the temptation: "Examine the environment in which you made your choice and ask what could have been done to make your choice making different." The man had, in fact, placed himself in a situation that made it easier to make bad choices. If he had avoided the situation, he could have resisted the temptation.

Several guidelines may be helpful as you attempt to avoid situations that test your self-control and challenge your willpower.

Identify your vulnerabilities. Try to learn your own weaknesses—those conditions that tempt you most. **What are your vulnerabilities?**

_____

_____

Once you know your weak points, you can begin to confront them.

Avoid obvious temptations. Determine what stimuli and settings tempt you to sin. Ask yourself, *When is my guard down?* **What are your temptations?**

_____

_____

Do everything in your power to minimize your encounters with temptation.

Pray about inevitable situations. There are some tempting circumstances you are unable to escape. **What are your inevitable situations?**

_____

_____

When you are unable to avoid a person or setting that is tempting, seek God's power through prayer to protect yourself from the inevitable temptations.

Confront problems as they occur. Don't accept small compromises in your life that will distort your judgment. **What problems must you confront?**

_____

_____

As sin in your life becomes apparent, seek God's forgiveness immediately and turn from your sin.

Affirm your relationships with God and others daily. The reaffirmation of your relationship to God and to loved ones strengthens your own resolve. **How can you affirm your relationships to God and others?**

_____

_____

Remind your family and friends of your love regularly, demonstrating your love in actions.

I have practiced some of these guidelines in my own life. Food, especially sweets, is one of my greatest weaknesses. So even though I entertain often, I try not to keep desserts in our house, and I give away any desserts left over from functions. I am also prone to negative thoughts about others, so I quote Scripture when those ungodly thoughts begin. I enjoy movies, but I know that many are inappropriate for a Christian. So, my husband and I have made the decision not to see any R-rated movies. I can sometimes speak harsh words to others. So, I have learned to say, "I'm sorry," and mean it. These are just a few of the specific ways I try to create more ideal conditions for my self-control.

If you do not have an ideal environment for self-control, begin to build it yourself. Follow these five guidelines and flee from temptation. Seek ideal conditions so you can be disciplined in your Christian life. Jesus taught us in the Model Prayer how to avoid sinful circumstances — *"And do not bring us into temptation, but deliver us from the evil one"* (Matthew 6:13). You should turn from evil and turn toward good. Don't go places where sin abounds. Create an atmosphere of holiness that will encourage self-control. Then you will have done your part to create ideal conditions.

Lifestyle Changes

Gardening is one of my favorite pastimes, though I don't get to work in the yard often. I love for my window boxes to bloom and my flowerbeds to blossom. It is hard to provide the perfect conditions consistently for hearty growth — fertile soil, adequate rain, and proper sunlight. Professional gardeners often build hothouses to ensure ideal conditions for the plants. God calls His children to create a "hothouse effect," ensuring personal growth through disciplined living. Self-control will help you protect yourself and create a more ideal environment.

Personal commitment, ideal conditions, and lifestyle changes are necessary for spiritual growth. Believers who desire to grow in the likeness of Christ need to utilize their own willpower. In addition to a personal commitment and ideal condition, each person must make some lifestyle changes. A godly lifestyle not only projects a positive witness in the world, but it promotes lasting self-discipline. Ungodly habits, attitudes, and behaviors must be replaced with godly ones. Jesus' lifestyle is an example to us — He possessed godly attitudes, disciplined habits, and unselfish behaviors. With the help of the Lord, we can make these lifestyle changes and adopt a lifestyle of godliness.

Dallas Willard gave instructions for a godly lifestyle in his book, *The Spirit of the Disciplines*.

My central claim is that we can become like Christ by doing one thing—by following him in the overall style of life he chose for himself. If we have faith in Christ, we must believe that he knew how to live. We can, through faith and grace, become like Christ by practicing the types of activities he engaged in, by arranging our whole lives around the activities he himself practiced in order to remain constantly at home in the fellowship of His Father.

We must study the life of Christ as recorded in Scripture in order to duplicate His lifestyle. If you trust Jesus Christ with your life, then you must trust Him with your lifestyle!

How would you describe your lifestyle? Compare your lifestyle to the lifestyle of Christ. Read Luke 4:1–15 to be reminded of how Jesus lived and ministered. Answer yes or no to the following questions and then explain your response:

Is your lifestyle like Christ's?

In your attitudes ___ yes ___ no. Why? _____

_____

In your habits ___ yes ___ no. Why? _____

_____

In your behaviors ___ yes ___ no. Why? _____

_____

Write a description of your present lifestyle. Then explain what can you do to improve it?

_____

_____

Making these lifestyle changes is not easy. Some personal willpower and daily discipline is necessary. The best lesson in self-control comes from Jesus Himself. He was always prepared for His work. He was devoted to prayer and Bible study. His lifestyle evidenced His love, care, and concern. Jesus received His Father's constant and effective support while doing His will. Jesus made the necessary changes to maintain a righteous lifestyle.

Let me tell you something about myself—I am not a "morning person." My husband, Chuck, wakes up every morning with a smile on his face. I wake up slowly, with great effort, and with more of a snarl than a smile. In fact, Chuck says that I don't even believe in God until ten o'clock in the morning! Each evening I try to go to bed early enough to get up the next morning on time. I love to stay up late, but I need eight hours of sleep. What a dilemma! Every night I must use self-control to force myself to go to bed. And every morning I must use even more self-discipline to get myself out of bed. (Most of the time my sweet husband is my alarm clock.) While I don't have the power to adjust my body clock, I do have the ability to exert my personal willpower. I must make a commitment to an early bedtime. I must create ideal conditions—turning off the television, taking a bubble bath, listening to soothing music. And I must make these changes a part of my lifestyle by repeating them every day.

God can strengthen us to be more disciplined. Paul's letter to Timothy affirms this promise: *"For God has not given us a spirit of fearfulness, but one of power, love, and sound judgment"* (2 Timothy 1:7). The Lord adds to my finite willpower His infinite power so I can be disciplined. You, too, have that power. You have your power to commit, and you have His power to change!

My Personal Discipline

The first step of divine discipline is personal willpower. Write below a prayer of personal commitment. Promise God that you will use your own power to lead a godly, disciplined life.

_____

_____

_____

_____

Dear Lord:
Thank You for giving me the power to control my life. Help me to
make a personal commitment, to create ideal conditions, and to
make lifestyle changes as I learn to be self-disciplined. Amen.

Lesson 6
Supernatural Godpower for Discipline

Divine Instruction

No temptation has overtaken you except what is common to humanity. God is faithful and He will not allow you to be tempted beyond what you are able, but with the temptation He will also provide a way of escape, so that you are able to bear it. — 1 Corinthians 10:13

A friend of mine recently complained that his stressful life was almost more than he could bear. (We have all probably felt that way at times.) I tried to gently encourage him with the words of Scripture — God never allows us to experience any more than we can handle, and He promises to help us bear it. My paraphrase of 1 Corinthians 10:13 was intended as a reminder of God's power to face life's challenges when we feel powerless. Though we must use our personal willpower, we become immediately aware of our inadequacies. Christians must be consciously aware of the supernatural power of God within them to resist temptation and withstand challenges.

While the first step in the process of divine discipline is personal willpower, for the believer the next step is God's supernatural power. *My power plus His power is truly divine discipline.* **Read the following paraphrase of 2 Corinthians 12:9–10 and insert your name in the blanks. Claim these verses as divine promises for God's power to be disciplined:**

My grace is sufficient for power is perfected in weakness. Therefore _____ will most gladly boast all the more about my weaknesses so that Christ's power may reside in me. So _____ takes pleasure in weaknesses, unsults, catastrophes, and in pressures, because of Christ. For when _____ is weak, then _____ is strong.

What a wonderful promise to know that the supernatural power of God is available to us! When we are at our weakest, God's power strengthens us. We can face any trial or temptation knowing that His power is able to overcome all obstacles. We can brag about our weaknesses because His strength triumphs over our inadequacies.

Paul was reminded of the awesome power of God working in his life to endure his thorn in the flesh. Sometimes it is easier to Grasp God's grace intellectually than to experience it personally. God reminded Paul often of His grace. In his weakness, Paul was strengthened by the Spirit. In our weakness, He also makes us strong. We can claim God's power to bear all thorns in our lives.

Some years ago, my husband Chuck received a telephone message that changed his life. The simple sentence, "Your father has had a heart attack," turned an ordinary day upside down. As Chuck drove the five hours to his hometown, uncertain of his father's condition, God's power began to work in his life. In his moments of human weakness, God strengthened Chuck with the promises of His Word. As the miles passed, he recalled Scriptures of hope. These Scriptures, learned in days past, became a present help!

> *"Do not fear, for I am with you; do not be afraid, for I am your God. I will strengthen you; I will help you; I will hold on to you with My righteous right hand."*
> —Isaiah 41:10

> *Humble yourselves therefore under the mighty hand of God, so that He may exalt you in due time, casting all your care upon Him, because He cares about you.*
> —1 Peter 5:6–7

> *I am able to do all things through Him who strengthens me.*
> —Philippians 4:13

God's Word strengthened Chuck, and His power healed Chuck's father who lived for many more years.

That same power is available to you. If you take the first step—use your own personal willpower—He promises to add His supernatural Godpower. He has done that throughout history as He has worked in the lives of His children, and He is doing it today in our lives. His power is available to us if we will simply tap its source.

God has chosen to share His supernatural power with you and me. It is our privilege to receive and experience His power. God's divine power is the active force that makes self-control in our lives possible. Personal willpower is not enough. We must accept God's power in order to face challenges, resist temptations, and live abundant lives. The believer must learn to practice His presence, claim His power, and seek His joy in this journey toward divine discipline.

His Presence

Have you ever been profoundly aware of the presence of the Lord in your life? Have you ever experienced His inexplicable power in your life? In your weakest moments, God's power is felt to be the strongest. I am grateful to say that I have often been aware of God's presence. When alone at home, I sense His presence and protection. When traveling alone, I am conscious of His presence and companionship. When I face illness, I am strengthened by His presence and healing power.

In 2002, I traveled to China with a group of 16 women for a two-week missions trip. While I was confident that God had opened that door for ministry, I became increasingly anxious as the departure date neared. In my weakness I asked myself why I would travel alone halfway across the world. I worried about health since I was recovering from major surgery. I feared the unknown details, wondering if I was adequately prepared to serve the Lord and facilitate the group. Though a devoted follower of the Lord, I was almost paralyzed by fear at the thought of going to a foreign country all alone. My husband helped me face my personal weakness and trust the strength of God. He prayed with me and for me. He wrote me daily Scriptures of promise. As I journeyed 30 hours to China, my first verse said: *"Haven't I commanded you: be strong and courageous? Do not be afraid or discouraged, for the LORD your God is with you wherever you go"* (Joshua 1:9). From the moment I read that promise until now, I have been keenly aware of God's presence with me. The same

God who promises to be with us in our homes is also with us on the other side of the earth. I have never felt His presence like I did on the planes, in the streets, and doing His work in China.

Read the following verses and determine what they say about the presence of God.

2 Chronicles 6:18 _____

Psalm 121:1–8 _____

Isaiah 40:21–23 _____

Jeremiah 23:23–24 _____

John 1:1–18 _____

1 Corinthians 6:19–20 _____

Ephesians 4:6 _____

Throughout Scripture God's presence is confirmed. There is no place without God, no place beyond Him (2 Chronicles 6:18). God is present in all of creation and in the lives of His people. He never sleeps or slumbers (Psalm 121:1–8). God is actively at work in the lives of His creation (Isaiah 40:21–23). God is not sequestered in a temple; He is with His children, near at hand (Jeremiah 23:23–24). From the beginning, God has existed and will exist forever. His presence is eternal (John 1:1–18). The Holy Spirit lives within the body of the believer (1 Corinthians 6:19–20). God is *above all*, *through all*, and *in all* (Ephesians 4:6). He is omnipresent for all eternity.

The Lord is present in the lives of His children, but He is not a conscious part of the unbeliever's life. Concerning the Holy Spirit, Jesus Himself said: *"And I will ask the Father, and He will give you another Counselor to be with you forever. He is the Spirit of truth. The world is unable to receive Him because it doesn't see Him or know Him. But you do know Him, because He remains with you and will be in you. I will not leave you as orphans; I am coming to you"* (John 14:16–18). What a precious promise to know that the Holy Spirit is with us now and forever!

The Holy Spirit is present permanently in the lives of all believers from the moment of salvation. He abides with you, dwells in you, and comes to you forever. God's presence is at work in His children. While the Father is God ruling over us and the Son is God acting for us, the Holy Spirit is God living within us. We can experience the full work of the Trinity in our lives daily.

Jesus explained His presence to His followers in the Gospel recorded by John: *"The one who believes in Me, as the Scripture has said, will have streams of living water flow from deep within him"* (John 7:38). The presence of God should flow through the lives of all believers. If the river of His Spirit is not flowing through you, there may be "rocks in your river." Sin may be blocking the flow of the Spirit through you. An undisciplined life gradually dims your awareness of the presence of God.

My husband has a powerful sermon entitled "Rocks in the River." As he preaches, Chuck reminds believers of the barriers built up by sin, which stop the flow of the Spirit in our lives. Scripture exhorts us to confess our sin so that the Spirit can work again (1 John 1:9). If you are not consciously aware of the presence of God, you may be hindered by sin. Gradually sin can stifle the work of God in your life. Confess your sin and accept God's forgiveness. Then God's presence will be experienced in your life again. God's presence will strengthen and comfort you.

God wants you to experience His present, His special gift to each believer. He wants you to receive the present of His presence—a gift of grace. Then He wants you to live constantly in His presence. In her book, *Don't Miss the Blessing*, JoAnn Leavell challenges her readers to "practice the presence of God." She suggests that four spiritual disciplines are necessary to truly feel His presence—regular worship, silence (meditation), daily Bible reading, and prayer. These spiritual disciplines are vehicles through which God's presence flows. God's presence promotes daily discipline, and discipline reveals His presence.

Do you experience the presence of God in your life daily? How faithfully do you practice these spiritual disciplines? Are these disciplines a permanent part of your everyday life? Honestly assess yourself in light of each spiritual discipline.

Place a check mark by the most accurate description of your spiritual discipline in each area.

Regular Worship
___ Not disciplined ___ Somewhat disciplined ___ Very disciplined

Meditation/Silence
___ Not disciplined ___ Somewhat disciplined ___ Very disciplined

Daily Bible Reading
___ Not disciplined ___ Somewhat disciplined ___ Very disciplined

Prayer
___ Not disciplined ___ Somewhat disciplined ___ Very disciplined

If you honestly confessed a lack of discipline in your spiritual life, then spend some time with God in confession and repentance. You should then be aware of the presence of God and begin again to practice His presence through these spiritual disciplines.

My granddaddy Harrington, a Methodist preacher, taught me a life-changing lesson about practicing the presence of God. After my grandmother's death, I went for a visit with him. We went out to eat at his favorite restaurant, and he asked for a table to seat four people. I knew there were only two of us, but he requested a table for four. During the meal, my precious grandfather explained why he always sat at a table with four chairs: "People think I must be lonely since I live all by myself. But I am not. When I go out to eat, I sit at a table for four so there is a chair for *me*, a chair for my *mama*, a chair for *Ludie* (his wife of 50-plus years), and a chair for the *Holy Spirit*. The four of us have a great time!" My grandfather practiced the presence of the Holy Spirit, and he taught his family to experience God's presence too.

Every believer should be practicing the presence of God. The Holy Spirit is always present. As a believer, you must be aware of His presence. Then you will be empowered by Him. Claim His supernatural power, and seek His joy.

His Power

God's presence encourages, His power strengthens! The Bible affirms the eternal presence of God. It also attests the power of God. God is described as all-powerful—omnipotent (Job 42:2; Psalm 135:6; Revelation 19:6). He is the sovereign ruler of the universe (Psalm 33:9; Psalm 66:7; Ephesians 4:6). He is the source of His own power (Psalm 21:13; Psalm 93:1; Isaiah 26:4).

God's power is on display for all to see in His creation and in His creatures (Psalm 19:1–4; Psalm 77:14; Psalm 111:6). His power is beyond human understanding (Job 37:5; Isaiah 55:8–11; Ephesians 3:20).

Before we examine the power of God, determine if you understand the meaning of His sovereignty.

Define the word *sovereign* in clear and simple words.

The word *sovereign* is an important doctrinal term. Though we cannot fully understand the sovereignty of God, we must respect it and accept it. *Merriam-Webster's* dictionary defines *sovereignty* as "supreme power or an example of supreme excellence." The *Holman Bible Dictionary* explains that *sovereignty* means that God is in all and over all. Therefore, the Bible teaches that God is the source of all creation and that all things come from and depend upon God.

Dallas Willard tried to describe the supernatural power of God in his book, *The Spirit of the Disciplines*. He concluded that "spiritual disciplines enable us more and more to live in a power that is, strictly speaking, beyond us, deriving from the spiritual realm itself." The power of God is more than we can comprehend and more than we can achieve personally. Christians must learn how to claim the power of God.

Have you ever experienced the supernatural power of God personally in your life? Recall a time and summarize your encounter in the space provided below.

There have been many times in my life when I have been strengthened supernaturally by the Holy Spirit. As I look back on those experiences, it is extremely clear that it was not my power but God's power enabling me to accomplish those fetes.

Some years ago when Papa Kelley became ill, Chuck's parents needed to move from Beaumont to Dallas, Texas. He was hospitalized there for cancer surgery and required chemotherapy and radiation. The move was necessary but they were unable to manage the move themselves. It was an overwhelming task to sell their home of 40 years, pack up and move their possessions, buy a new house, and settle their belongings. But, God called me to move them, and He promised to help me. As I reflect back on that time, it is so apparent that God had gone before us preparing the way. The house sold in a matter of days. Selected sentimental items were distributed to family and friends, and personal possessions were moved to the new home. Everything was settled in the same places according to photographs taken. When the Kelleys walked into their new home, their surroundings were familiar. It was a huge job, but I didn't accomplish it alone. God empowered me, family assisted me, and friends encouraged me. His supernatural power was my strength.

How can you receive the power of God? While there are many ways to claim His power, the most effective method is prayer. As we pray, God releases His power in us. Don't underestimate the power of prayer! In fact, begin to utilize God's power through prayer.

What is prayer? Prayer is not a one-way monologue of requests to God. It is not a soliloquy of disappointments in life. Instead, prayer is a two-way conversation between the Father and His child. It is a heavenly dialogue. Many believers fail to understand the true meaning of prayer. Thus, they miss out on the power of God. Self-discipline is needed to experience the power of prayer.

If there is such power in prayer, why don't Christians pray? John Stott, a dynamic British preacher, answered that question in a sermon preached at All Souls Church in London. He spoke of the great paradox of prayer. A part of us wants to pray because of the joy in praying. But a part of us doesn't want to pray because of the conviction in praying. According to Stott, we must win the "battle of the threshold." We must discipline ourselves to pray so that God can empower us.

Stott clarified this phrase, "battle of the threshold," with an illustration. Imagine that God is within a walled garden. The devil stands in the only doorway, trying to stop you from approaching God. Each time you enter the presence of God through prayer, you must pass through the gate guarded by Satan. Only when you win the "battle of the threshold" can you get through to God and receive His power. It takes discipline to cross the threshold, to defeat the enemy. But the effort is worth it. The victorious believer is empowered by God to face all of life's challenges.

The Bible discusses the power of God. It clearly states that God's power in the believer overcomes all temptation. **Find 1 Corinthians 10:13 in your Bible and read it carefully. Answer the questions below based on the meaning of the text.**

Who provides the power? _____

_____

Who receives the power? _____

_____

How does He give the power? _____

_____

Why does He give the power? _____

_____

God alone is the source of all power. He offers His power to all His children if we will receive it. God gives the power through His Spirit, working in the lives of faithful believers. And God gives the power to help us overcome every temptation, no matter how great or how small.

During trials and temptation, God's power is available to His children. You can win any battle and conquer all hardship if you seek His power through prayer. Self-control is possible by the power of the Holy Spirit! The believer can practice God's presence and claim His power. You can also pursue His joy!

His Joy

God wants to give us His presence and His power. He also wants us to experience His joy! God desires for His children to live an abundant life, filled with joy and blessings. His joy is not fleeting or dependent on circumstances. His joy is unending and is unconditional. You will find self-control obtainable if you seek spiritual joy.

Thomas Aquinas is credited with this quote in the book, *The Wisdom of the Saints*: "No one can live without delight, and that is why a man deprived of spiritual joy goes over to carnal pleasures." God created us with a desire for happiness. He wants us to know joy and pleasure, but not apart from Him. A Christian who is not experiencing the "joy of her salvation" will seek pleasure in other ways. Through divine discipline, we can have the joy of the Lord.

You may ask, "What is spiritual joy?" It is the complete satisfaction that comes from knowing God. It is a deep feeling of happiness regardless of the circumstances. Joy is not the result of my own control. It is confidence in God, for He controls everything! Since God is in control, He brings me joy in all things. Paul said it this way in Romans 8:28: *"We know that all things work together for the good of those who love God: those who are called according to His purpose."* True joy is enjoyed by the believer who seeks God's will in all things.

Christmas has just passed, and it was a time of true joy for me and my family. We all gathered in New Orleans and enjoyed sweet times together. It was not a time of joy because of our extravagant presents or perfect lives. In fact, due to the economic challenges, the gifts were smaller than usual. There were a few family squabbles with so many people involved. And, there was sorrow because it was the first Christmas without my dad's wife, Becky, who died suddenly this year. But, each of us experienced true joy in Jesus, the reason for the season. We thanked God for the gift of His Son, and reflected on our many blessings.

Like self-control, joy is part of the fruit of the Holy Spirit (Galatians 5:22–23). Joy is a blessing from God, an evidence of His work in us. Spiritual joy gives strength (Nehemiah 8:10). Spiritual joy should also characterize every believer. Augustine of Hippo, a fourth-century theologian, said: "The Christian should be an alleluia from head to foot!" The joy of the Lord should naturally flow from the life of a believer.

Hannah Whitall Smith wrote an inspiring book about spiritual joy in the late 1800s. In *The Christian's Secret of a Happy Life*, she encouraged Christians to seek His joy: "Joy comes through obedience to Christ, and joy results from obedience to Christ. Without obedience, joy is hollow and artificial." Joy depends on discipline and discipline leads to joy. Seek spiritual joy!

Spiritual joy is very different from earthly pleasures. Not only is it eternal, it is personal. The primary theme of Paul's letter to the **Philippians is joy. On fifteen occasions Paul emphasizes joy as a blessing of faithfulness. Read these verses in the Book of Philippians and note the theme of joy.**

Philippians 1:4 — _____ with joy

Philippians 1:18 — in _____ I rejoice

Philippians 1:25 — joy of _____

Philippians 1:26 — rejoice for _____

Philippians 2:2 — _____ my joy

Philippians 2:17 — rejoice in your _____

Philippians 2:27 — rejoice and be less _____

Philippians 3:1 — rejoice in the _____

Philippians 4:1 — my joy and _____

Philippians 4:4 — rejoice in the Lord _____

Paul's theme of joy is apparent in the Book of Philippians. He concludes his letter with instructions on how to receive God's joy (Philippians 4:8): Think on these things—

> Whatever is *true*,
> Whatever is *honorable*,
> Whatever is *just*,
> Whatever is *pure*,
> Whatever is *lovely*,
> Whatever is *commendable*,
> If there is any *moral excellence* and if there is any *praise*—dwell on these things.

In this verse, Paul gives a prescription for joy. He identifies things we are to *think*, things we are to *do*, and things we are to *receive*. **Read the entire passage in Philippians 4:8–9 and list those things below.**

Things to *Think* (verse 8): _____

Things to *Do* (verse 9*a*): _____

Things to *Receive* (verse 9*b*): _____

A believer will experience indescribable joy if she thinks about things that are true, honorable, just, pure, lovely, and commendable. Virtuous thoughts give joy. If you study, receive, hear, see, and do these things, you will be filled with His joy. As you pursue godliness, you receive the peace of God. What a blessing to practice His presence, claim His power, and seek His joy!

Anne Ortlund, a well-known Christian author and speaker, wrote about the Holy Spirit's work in her life in her book, *The Disciplines of the Heart*: "The light of God surrounds me; the love of God enfolds me; the power of God protects me; the presence of God watches over me; wherever I am, God is."

How would you describe the work of the Holy Spirit in your life? Complete the sentences below in your own words and be

thankful for God's everlasting presence, supernatural power, and indescribable joy.

The light of God_____me;

The love of God _____me;

The power of God _____me;

The presence of God _____me;

Wherever I am, God is.

In this lesson, we have examined the second step in divine discipline—supernatural Godpower. Once you have committed your personal willpower, you can receive the power of God to be disciplined. While personal willpower is limited, God's power is an unlimited source of strength. When you depend on Godpower, His presence will encourage you, His power will strengthen you, and His joy will sustain you. You should be motivated to live a disciplined life! But you can also add to your power and His power the power of other people. That will be the focus of our next chapter. So be determined in your divine discipline!

My Personal Discipline

Choose one of the following Psalms that proclaim God's power. Write a paraphrase of the verse below. Memorize the verse and prepare to experience supernatural Godpower!

Psalm 27:1   **Psalm 28:7**   **Psalm 46:1**

_____

_____

_____

_____

Dear Lord:
I am ready to use my personal willpower, but I also need Your super-natural Godpower. I claim Your presence to encourage, Your power to strengthen, and Your joy to sustain. Amen.

Lesson 7
People's Persuasive Power for Discipline

Divine Instruction
Therefore encourage one another and build each other up as you are already doing. — 1 Thessalonians 5:11

People can exert great power on other people—the power to help or hurt, encourage or discourage, build up or tear down. In addition to personal willpower and supernatural Godpower, Christians can turn to people for their persuasive power in the pursuit of self-control. The positive influence of others can strengthen resolve and develop discipline. The power of people is very apparent.

The most obvious example of people's persuasive power is seen in teenagers. Because they desperately want to be accepted, teens are greatly influenced by peer pressure. Young people want to look and act like their friends. They want to wear blue jeans, but not just any jeans—only the brand or style of jeans worn by their friends. They want their hair to look like their friends, but not just any hairstyle—the trendy one. Teenagers are greatly influenced by their peers.

Adults are also influenced by others. Personal friends and famous people have persuasive power over us. Whether they intend to or not, Christians are affected by the lifestyles of other people. There is an innate desire to "keep up with the Joneses"—to have as nice a car and house and clothes. Because of the natural persuasive power of people, it is important to be surrounded by godly friends and Christian role models. Their influence will be positive and divine discipline will be promoted.

In recent years, the United States and even the world have faced serious economic problems. Many of the financial woes of people and companies have been based on the desire to keep up with others. Individuals desire more money or more expensive cars even when they cannot afford them. Families want larger houses and finer schools even when they live above their means. Businesses seek to compete with other businesses so they spend more on advertising and bonuses. Therefore, people and companies today find themselves facing financial woes. The rising debt is due in great part to the inherent desire to be like others. As Christians, we must control the desires to imitate others and instead imitate Him. We must be satisfied with our lives and circumstances, knowing that God has our best interest in mind. And, we must imitate only good and godly people.

Christians can look to the Bible for godly examples. Many men and women in the Scripture lived faithfully. They can have powerful influence on us today. Numerous women of the Bible have guided my life. At different stages of my life, specific personal stories have challenged me. As a Christian woman, I am influenced by the unwavering faith of Hannah (1 Samuel 2:1–10). As a committed wife, I am affected by the total devotion of the virtuous woman (Proverbs 31:10–31). And as a women's leader, I am persuaded by the leadership ability of Deborah (Judges 4:4–14).

Which women of the Bible have influenced you personally? Why?

_____

_____

Christians can also be influenced by godly friends. People who live out their faith in unselfish service can make a powerful impact on others.

Whom do you admire? Whom do you try to imitate? List their names below and some of their positive traits you would like to develop.

_____

_____

I can think of several Christian friends who have influenced my life. In my childhood, the faith of my mother and both of my grandmothers profoundly impacted me. I am so grateful for my godly heritage!

As a teenager, I was strongly influenced by a lovely young woman named Beth, who was dedicated to the Lord. As a college student, I looked up to the sponsor of my service organization who was a devoted wife. As a seminary student wife, I followed the example of the president's wife, who used her spiritual gifts to minister to others. All of these Christian women and many more have made a difference in my life for the good. If we will find godly role models, their persuasive power can help us develop divine discipline.

In the journey toward self-control, personal willpower and supernatural Godpower are essential. However, we also need the persuasive power of other people. Godly friends can nurture and understand as well as evaluate and affirm. Their encouragement can strengthen the disciple and support the discipline. My husband and I would probably be unable to survive the demands of our hectic lives without the support of other people. In addition, without others, life has less meaning. We must depend on others for *acceptance, affirmation*, and *accountability* in our pursuit of divine discipline.

Acceptance

One of the most important qualities of friendship is acceptance. If a person accepts you unconditionally, she may become a dear friend. Without understanding, a friendship cannot be sustained. The Book of Proverbs says that a true friend *"loves at all times"* (Proverbs 17:17). Acceptance is the foundation for love in all relationships. Without acceptance between partners, a marriage is doomed. To be accepted and to accept others is helpful in the quest of divine discipline.

Jesus taught His followers about acceptance in His encounter with an adulterous woman. The scribes and Pharisees shunned the immoral woman who was caught in the act of adultery. Jesus responded in love to the woman. When questioned by the religious leaders, he asked the woman's accusers to judge her. They couldn't. They were convicted by their own intolerance. Those who rejected the sinful woman learned to accept her. Their acceptance encouraged her and strengthened them.

Turn in your Bible to the Gospel of John. Read this disciple's account of Jesus' acceptance and forgiveness of the adulterous

woman in John 8:1–12. Explain why it was so important for the Christians to accept the sinner.

_____

_____

God extends His love and forgiveness to all. Even the most sinful person is accepted by God, who knows the power of salvation to redeem and restore. Followers of Christ today must accept others — all others. Though it is difficult to love the unlovable, God's love will reach out unconditionally through us. Acceptance of others may draw them to the Savior, and acceptance of others will encourage them to be disciplined.

In recent months a group of young women in our church and at the seminary have begun to reach out to women in the French Quarter of New Orleans. It has been awesome to see God change the hearts of these precious Christian women, giving them a love and concern for those women living in sin. No longer judging or condemning them, the ladies of Inward Ministry care for them and pray for them as sisters or friends. Under different circumstances, the dancers and strippers could be their college roommates or their colleagues at work. They are about the same age, but live such different lives. God has been doing a work of redemption in many of them as they are accepted and loved in Christ. God is working through the commitment of His followers to influence unbelievers to faith in Jesus Christ. Divine discipline can be encouraged by the godly examples of others.

When I first began my search for self-control, God convicted me about my eating. My weight was out of control. I made the commitment of my personal willpower and turned to God for His supernatural power. But I also needed the persuasive power of other people. I was grateful for their acceptance of me even in my overweight condition. However, I was greatly strengthened when they also accepted my determination to be disciplined. Their love and concern for me kept me going.

In any area of your life, the acceptance of friends can strengthen you. They can understand you even if they don't face the same challenges. My friend, Sandra, has never been overweight in her life. But she understood my need to control my eating. She encouraged me and helped me along the way. When eating out, she ate a salad with me. She exercised with me and celebrated my loss of weight. Her unconditional love and acceptance supported me in my pursuit of personal discipline.

Do you have friends or family members who extend to you their full acceptance? Take a few moments to reflect on the influence of others on your life. Also, make the time to write them a note of gratitude, thanking them for their love and understanding. Write the names here of those people to whom you will write a note of thanks.

_____

_____

The Lord wants you to remember the acceptance of others.

I am so humbled by the love and concern expressed to me by many people. So many wonderful people have invested themselves in my life through the years. It is hard to express my appreciation and love. But, there is a song that speaks the words of my heart. In fact, I cry tears of gratitude every time I hear the words of the Ray Boltz song—"Thank you for giving to the Lord, I am a life that was changed. Thank you for giving to the Lord, I am so glad you gave."

God smiles when His children are accepted by others for who we are. He also desires for us to give unselfish acceptance to others. It is impossible to minister to others in Jesus' name without accepting love. **How sensitive are you to the needs of others? Are you aware of the burdens of family and friends? Do you accept all people, even the difficult ones, as children of God, loved by Him, and needing your care? List below some people you have chosen to accept even though they are different and sometimes challenging.**

_____

_____

Be obedient to your Father by extending love and acceptance to all of His children. Try to follow the Golden Rule: "*Whatever you want other sto do for you, do also the same for them*" (Matthew 7:12). Accept others as you would have them accept you.

A psychologist friend of mine encourages parents to love children for who they are and not what they do. It is much easier to affirm good behaviors than to accept the person herself. Human love and acceptance is typically based on conditions, desired behaviors. God's acceptance is focused on the individual, not the behavior. Are you grateful that God accepts you for yourself? Are you blessed when others accept you? Then offer that personal acceptance to others. Acceptance is powerful and persuasive. The *acceptance* of others fosters self-control. The *affirmation* of others also promotes personal discipline.

Affirmation

Affirmation is a natural result of acceptance. When you accept individuals unconditionally, you are eager to offer them praise and encouragement. Words of appreciation will flow from the mouths of accepting persons. The words of affirmation will minister comfort and strength to the receiver. Positive comments can contribute to a person's self-control.

Exhortation or encouragement is a spiritual gift, a special ability given by God to some people to lift up others. Many Christians have the gift of exhortation. Aren't we glad? I am grateful for the precious people who encourage me. Their words of affirmation bring me joy and strengthen my personal discipline. The ladies enrolled in the Women's Ministry Program at the New Orleans Baptist Theological Seminary are such encouragers to me! They give gifts of gratitude and write notes of affirmation. I keep those notes for future encouragement. I am strengthened when I reach into my "joy box" and reread their words of love. I am also motivated to affirm others by writing notes.

Are you grateful? Do you speak words of thanks? Do you write words of appreciation? Formulate several statements of appreciation that you can share with others. Write five sentences of affirmation and plan to use them.

1. _____

2. _____

3. _____

4. _____

5. _____

It is hard to teach children the discipline of letter writing. In fact, adults must be disciplined to write notes too. The art of letter writing has been lost today. But with discipline, this art of affirmation can be revived. Don't let spoken words of thanks suffice! The written word can be read and reread. The affirmation continues. It illustrates that the words of another person are powerful, influencing us through affirmation.

Mom Kelley has the spiritual gift of letter writing! Every Monday she writes 25 to 30 cards or notes to encourage friends and family members. She writes to everyone in her Sunday School class who was absent that week. She writes a family letter (called "the pink letter" because of the pink stationery) and sends it to 12 different addresses. She mails birthday and anniversary cards as well as sympathy and get-well cards. Her letter-writing ministry has touched many people. In fact, several church members have stated that they resumed attending church because of her correspondence. She lovingly accepts people and affirms them with words of encouragement.

The Bible records many people who were encouragers. Barnabas, whose name literally means "son of encouragement," is an inspiring example of affirmation. In Acts 11:19–28, his support of the Christians in Antioch is recorded. He was glad to see them and encouraged them in their work (v. 23). He was a good man, full of the Holy Spirit and of faith (v. 24). The positive spirit of Barnabas strengthened the young believers in the Lord and influenced others to faith in Him. Your words of affirmation can impact others, and their words of affirmation can affect you.

In 1 Thessalonians 5:11, Paul instructed believers to *"encourage one another and build each other up."* Affirmation is important to the body of Christ and it is a powerful instrument in discipline. Paul also told Christians to encourage their leaders. **Read 1 Thessalonians 5:12–15 as it is written below. Fill in the blanks with verbs of affirmation from the Scripture.**

Now we ask you, brothers, to give _____ to those who labor among you and lead you in the Lord and admonish you, and to _____ them very highly in love because of their work. Be at peace among yourselves. And we _____ you, brothers: warn those who are _____, comfort the _____, help those who are _____, be patient with _____. See to it that no one repays evil for evil to anyone, but always pursue what is good for one another and for all.

Paul includes numerous verbs of affirmation in this passage — recognize, regard, exhort, comfort, help, be patient. He describes the actions of others: irresponsible, discouraged, weak. He underscores the importance of affirmation by repetition and expansion. He feels strongly that affirmation is an important discipline with powerful impact on others. The apostle concludes this section of Scripture with a clear reminder — *"Rejoice always! Pray constantly. Give thanks in everything, for this is God's will for you in Christ Jesus"* (1 Thessalonians 5:16–18). It is God's will for us to affirm others and it is God's power that propels the affirmation.

My husband, Chuck, has the gift of encouragement. He is a great encourager to me and to many others. As a husband, he supports all that I do and praises my accomplishments. His many expressions of love affirm me and encourage me to practice self-control. As a leader, his public recognition of those working with him thrills them and motivates them to work harder. Affirmation is powerful. Encouragement greatly influences people. People wield persuasive power as they *accept* others, *affirm* them, and hold them *accountable.*

Accountability

Friends offer us acceptance and affirmation, but they also ensure accountability. Their unconditional love gives a feeling of belonging.

Their unselfish encouragement promotes a feeling of worth. And their unending observation fosters a feeling of responsibility. The persuasive power of people requires all three interactions and helps us develop self-control.

Accountability is the responsibility accepted for one's actions. A Christian is accountable to God for personal actions. A Christian is accountable to God for her behavior. She will be punished for unrighteousness and rewarded for righteousness. We are also accountable to others who want an explanation for our behavior. Accountability can motivate our pursuit of personal discipline.

In 1990, I wrote a personal testimony in my book, *Divine Discipline*. Since that time, I have had hundreds of opportunities to share that testimony with others. Each time, I become more accountable to live a disciplined life. Sometimes I wish God hadn't taught me that lesson because now He holds me accountable. At times I wish He didn't open doors for me to teach others this lesson because they hold me accountable. It seems that God knew that I needed a lot of accountability to practice divine discipline.

In what areas of your life do you need the accountability of others? Be specific as you list them below.

_____

_____

Most of us are more disciplined and improve our behavior if we have friends who hold us accountable. Thank God for their positive power in our lives!

Have you noticed the recent popularity of support groups? People seem to be strengthened by other people who have a similar experience or commitment. Support groups provide acceptance and affirmation plus accountability. Individuals sense belonging when a common need is shared and receive strength when a similar struggle is experienced. Group participation also holds each member responsible for action. Weight Watchers and Alcoholics Anonymous provide accountability to those who want to lose weight or stop drinking. Without peer pressure and group monitoring, self-control is more difficult. Weekly weigh-ins and daily activity logs encourage responsibility for behavior and achievement of goals.

In their book *Love Hunger*, Dr. Frank Minirth and his coauthors discuss the necessity of support groups for people recovering from food addiction. Outside encouragement is extremely helpful as food addicts control their eating. They benefit from the empathy of others. All of us benefit from the accountability of others.

Within the church, small groups become sources of peer accountability. Sunday School classes, Bible study groups, and prayer teams provide for spiritual growth but also hold members accountable for attendance and development. Many women are more disciplined in their Bible study when they participate in a Bible study group. They learn from others and enjoy fellowship when gathering, but they are also more apt to complete their home-work if they must report to others. People, including family and friends, provide accountability in our process of self-discipline.

Even a person who is in a very loving family relationship will need the fellowship of others, walkers who have been over the same paths they have been. People in your family are in one sense too close to your problem because of living with you, and in another sense too removed from it because they haven't experienced the same addiction. It is good to have Christian friends to support and encourage your personal and spiritual growth.

Personally, I need to be held accountable for my behavior. I am much more faithful in my Bible study when I teach a class for others or discuss my homework with friends. I am more disciplined in exercise if I attend aerobics or walk with a friend. For several years, I walked every morning with four friends. Their commitment made me accountable to exercise daily at 7:00 A.M. I learned that those who were absent were the topic of discussion. I showed up out of self-defense! My friends were my accountability for physical discipline. Accountability by others promotes my self-control. I am also motivated by my accountability to God. As His child, God is interested in my actions. He lovingly but firmly holds me account-able for my behavior.

The Bible reminds the Christian of her accountability to God. **Before each statement below write *true* or *false* to indicate the accuracy of the fact.**

_____ Each person will give a personal account to God.

_____ Each person will give an account for every care-less word spoken.

_____ Each person will give an account for all things.

Now read the following Scriptures which confirm these statements as true:

Romans 14:12
Matthew 12:36
Hebrews 4:13

Scripture acknowledges our accountability to God.

Every believer will one day stand before God to give a personal account for her life (Romans 14:12). Every believer will give God an account for every careless word spoken (Matthew 12:36). And every believer will give an account for every action (Hebrews 4:13). We are accountable to God for every behavior—He is our divine accountant, recording debts and credits in His ledger. We are accountable to others for certain behaviors—they are our human accountants, noting failures and successes. Accountability empowers discipline.

In another passage of the New Testament, the writer of Hebrews notes the significance of people's persuasive power. He exhorts all believers to accept and affirm each other as well as hold each other accountable. Hebrews 10:23–25 says:

> Let us hold on to the confession of our hope without wavering, for He who promised is faithful. And let us be concerned about one another in order to promote love and good works, not staying away from our meetings, as some habitually do, but encouraging each other, and all the more as you see the day drawing near.

Every believer is to be firm in faith, not wavering. That faithfulness is stimulated by fellowship with others.

The interaction with others stirs up love and good works. It is disappointing today to see many Christians uninvolved in church.

In fact, even seminary students, those called to full-time Christian ministry, sometimes fail to get involved in church. Because of their busy lives, they do not prioritize worship with other believers. Over time, the habit of church disappears. It is not surprising then that children stop going to church as they grow up. All Christians need the support and love of other Christians. So, do not miss out on assembling together with other believers. Encourage one another, especially as the return of Christ approaches.

Be persuaded positively by other people as you pursue personal discipline. Be strengthened by their acceptance, encouraged by their affirmation, and challenged by their accountability. Divine discipline will develop as you use your willpower, utilize His God-power, and understand their persuasive power. To make it effective and lasting, your divine discipline must be personalized.

My Personal Discipline

In another epistle, Paul admonished believers to encourage each other with kind words. Read the verse below, then reword it from your heart.

No rotten talk should come from your mouth, but only what is good for the building up of someone in need, in order to give grace to those who hear. —Ephesians 4:29

_____

_____

Memorize this Scripture as a reminder to always be an encouragement to other people.

Dear Lord:
Thank You for giving people persuasive power. Help me graciously receive their acceptance, affirmation, and accountability, and teach me to extend them to others. Amen.

Lesson 8
Personalized Discipline

Divine Instruction

Then He said to them all, "If anyone wants to come with Me, he must deny himself, take up his cross daily, and follow Me." — Luke 9:23

People are different. God created each individual with a unique personality and special qualities. It is necessary for each of us to understand who we are and how we function. Since we are so different from others, we cannot copy their successes and hope to succeed. We cannot attempt their accomplishments and become accomplished. We cannot duplicate their disciplines and act disciplined. Each of us must understand ourselves and personalize discipline.

While God affirms our worth and value, He also recognizes our differences. The Bible declares our value in God's eyes: *"But you are a chosen race, a royal priesthood, a holy nation, a people for His possession, so that you may proclaim the praises of the One who called you out of darkness into His marvelous light. Once you were not a people, but now you are God's people; you had not received mercy, but now you have received mercy"* (1 Peter 2:9–10). If you have ever doubted your significance or questioned your worthiness, you can be confident in your value to God. He created you uniquely and He loves you completely. His concern for you should strengthen your self-esteem, your feelings about yourself.

From the Scripture above, write the words that God uses to describe you in the spaces below. You are...

a _____ *race*
a _____ *priesthood*
a _____ *nation*
a people for His _____

God has created you perfectly and with a purpose. You are chosen, royal, holy, and special to Him. You are His possession and should proclaim His praises. You were created to proclaim the praises of the God who saved you. So you are valuable to God for *who* you are and *what* you do.

This Scripture passage is a great encouragement to me personally. When my relationships are strained, I remember that He chose me. When my appearance seems lacking, I recall that I am royal. When I make mistakes, He reminds me that I am holy. And when I feel rejected by others, I recognize that I am special. I am special to Him now and I will always be special to Him.

I first understood this truth as a young child when God chose me for salvation. After my father's dramatic conversion, I realized that I needed a personal relationship with Jesus. At the tender age of six, I knew God loved me and wanted to forgive me of my sins. I trusted Him as Savior though I did not fully understand all His teachings. I was baptized as a testimony of His work in my life. Since my conversion, I have grown in my faith and have remained close to Him. My salvation experience clearly indicates that I am chosen, royal, holy, and special in His sight.

As a teenager, God again chose me. He called me to special service. Though I was unsure of the particular ministry area, I knew that God wanted me to proclaim Him to others. He did not choose me because I was more capable or more spiritual than others. He chose me because I was willing—*"Here I am! Send me"* (Isaiah 6:8). I have been chosen by Him for salvation and for service. As I teach and speak and write, I declare His glory and draw people to Him. My personal call to Christian service is a joy to me and a blessing to others.

During college, I was again called. I was chosen by God to marry a very special man. When I met Chuck, I was attracted to his godly character and commitment to the Lord. We fell in love and planned to spend our lives together. God had definitely called each of us to salvation and to service as He also chose both of us for marriage. Throughout these 36 years, I have renewed my commitment to Chuck. My marriage has brought such pleasure to me and has been a witness of God's love to others.

In 1996, God called me again. When Chuck was elected president of the New Orleans Baptist Theological Seminary, I became the president's wife. Though I had not sought that position, God had prepared me for the position. All of my life experiences have equipped me to serve this important role. Chuck and I have been chosen by God to lead this precious school. We are humbled by His call and keenly aware of the responsibility. Of all my roles, there is no greater task than my work alongside my husband. On my business cards, I proudly proclaim my title as president's wife. My ministry at the seminary has been incredibly rewarding.

My testimony is personal—God has chosen me for salvation and service, for marriage and ministry. He created me uniquely and has set me apart for His purpose. He has also done that for you. God has chosen you and created you for a purpose.

Carefully consider your relationship to the Lord. Have you responded to His call to salvation? Have you surrendered your life to Christian service? Are you living a holy life? Do you feel His special concern?

Write a personal testimony of God's work in your life.

_____

_____

_____

_____

Personal discipline must develop after a personal decision to follow Christ and serve Him is made. Once you accept God's love and forgiveness, you must live for Him. You must confess your sin and seek to imitate His sinless life. You must understand who you are in Christ—chosen, royal, holy, special. But you must also recognize your limitations. You must discipline yourself daily to be godly.

Personal discipline requires personal evaluation. You must know your weaknesses and your vulnerabilities before you can overcome them. Honest self-evaluation is the first part of personalized discipline. When your weaknesses are clearly identified, you can set goals to overcome them, and then you can reward your accomplishments.

Identify Weaknesses

Because people are different, we have unique strengths and varied weaknesses. Each personality has traits that are positive and others that are negative. Our lifelong challenge is to honestly identify personal weaknesses. It is much easier to see the faults in others and overlook our own imperfections.

Jesus Himself questioned our hesitancy to judge ourselves: *"Why do you look at the speck in your brother's eye but don't notice the log in your own eye?"* (Matthew 7:3). Jesus knew our natural tendencies. Our human nature wants to notice the minor errors of others while ignoring our own major weaknesses. It is helpful to remember your worth to God while recognizing your own frailties.

It is definitely more comfortable to notice the failures in others and suggest changes that need to be made. However, we must point our fingers of accusation at ourselves first. My dad often said that while I am pointing my finger at someone else, there are four fingers pointing back at me. Leo Tolstoy, the great Russian writer, once said: "Everybody thinks of changing humanity, and nobody thinks of changing himself." Think about yourself—your own weaknesses. Then make some changes in your own life. As we change personally, we influence others to change.

Marriage provides a classic example of the desire to change others. A woman falls in love with a man, liking everything about him. As soon as the wedding ceremony is over, the eager wife tries to change everything she once loved about him. The words "I do" (take you as my husband) become "I will" (change you into the man of my dreams). The wife needs to change herself and not her husband.

As an enthusiastic young bride, I quickly learned there are some things about Chuck that I will never be able to change. (If you are married, I am sure that you have learned a similar lesson about your husband!) He has some irritating habits that will not change. I must accept the way he squeezes his toothpaste tube, eats his spaghetti, and loads the dishwasher. I must adjust my expectations and understand his differences. I can buy two tubes of toothpaste, give him a spoon for his spaghetti, and thank him for loading the dishwasher. I can change myself, but I cannot force change on my husband or other people. If I try to force change on others, it will strain the relationships.

Paul guided the Christians in Ephesus in their self-evaluation. He suggested that they contrast their old sinful natures with their new lives in Christ. Personal weaknesses often display themselves in sin and immorality. **Read Ephesians 4:17–24. List below some behaviors that contrast the "old man" and the "new man," weaknesses and strengths of character.**

Old Man (weaknesses)	New Man (strengths)
_____	_____
_____	_____
_____	_____
_____	_____

According to Paul, sin results in futility, darkness, alienation, ignorance, and blindness (verses 17–18). The sinner's life is characterized by lewdness, uncleanness, greediness, corruption, deceit, and lusts (verses 19–22). These ungodly behaviors are sins in the eyes of God and weaknesses in the lives of Christians. This corrupt conduct is to be taken off, put away (verse 23). The sinful behavior is to be replaced by godliness. The new creation is clothed in truth, righteousness, and holiness—strengths or virtues of obedient living (verse 24).

The Bible states that *"all have sinned and fall short of the glory of God"* (Romans 3:23). **In the next few minutes, examine your own weaknesses. What areas of your life need to be disciplined? List them below.**

_____

_____

_____

_____

Identifying your personal weaknesses is necessary before changes can be made. I have many weaknesses in my own life. They are apparent to me at some times more than others. But I must honestly evaluate my behavior before I can change it. At this time I am aware of these weaknesses:

I have not been consistent in my daily time with the Lord.
I have not been disciplined enough to exercise daily.
I have not been bold in my personal witness.
I have not been regular in my communication with friends.
I have not made time to straighten the clutter on my desk.

These are just a few of my personal weaknesses. Now that I have singled them out, I must seek to improve. I must set goals for achievement and discipline myself to reach them. You must personalize your discipline too! It is somewhat discouraging to identify your personal weaknesses. However, you cannot begin the process of change with the help of self-discipline without this important first step. You must periodically perform a check-up to recognize weaknesses and develop strengths. Ask the Lord to convict you of your sin and shortcomings then to strengthen you to overcome them and develop self-control. The next step in personalizing your discipline is to set some goals for yourself.

Set Goals

Specific action must be taken if you are to follow Christ. A Christian should set goals and clarify objectives for godly living. Self-discipline is necessary to accomplish these goals. Immature, carnal believers have no spiritual goals. Their lives just unfold daily without a purpose. Mature, godly believers have specific, spiritual goals. Their lives are filled with activities that fulfill their purposes of becoming more like Christ. Reasonable goals are needed for spiritual growth.

Let's consider what we mean by a "goal." A goal is simply a target for our behavior. It is a specific aim toward which an endeavor is directed. A goal is not a desire—it is a direction. JoAnn Leavell compares a goal and a desire in her book, *Don't Miss the Blessing*. She states, "A goal is something I want which I *can* control. A desire is something I want which I *cannot* control. A wish, on the other hand, is a desire without any subsequent effort." God would have us set reasonable goals for spiritual maturity—behaviors we can accomplish through disciplined living.

My personal tendency is to make wishes rather than set goals. I wish for many things in my life: "I wish I could lose weight." "I wish I had more money." "I wish I had more time to relax." Most of these thoughts are only desires. No change in behavior takes place when wishes are made. A wish depends on mere luck, while a goal requires hard work—discipline. I must set some specific goals in order to achieve my desired results. My goals could be: lose ten pounds, save $1000, or schedule one afternoon each week for relaxation.

Like me, you may have many different goals, many behaviors to change. Your challenge will be to identify the goal that needs work first. Determining priorities requires the leadership of the Lord. Keeping those priorities demands discipline. In her book, *Disciplines of a Beautiful Woman*, Anne Ortlund discusses establishment of priorities. She defines *lifelong priorities* (major goals to be accomplished in one's lifetime) and *daily priorities* (specific goals to be completed daily in order to fulfill lifelong priorities). In order to be productive you must determine several general long-term goals and some specific short-term goals. **Take time now to record those goals. Use these spaces below to write your personal objectives.**

Long-term goals: _____

_____

_____

Short-term goals: _____

_____

_____

Your long-term goals should give overall guidance to your life. Your short-term goals should dictate your daily activities.

Jesus taught about priorities in His encounter with Mary and Martha of Bethany. Martha was busy in the kitchen accomplishing her short-term objectives. Her sister, Mary, was sitting at the feet of Jesus fulfilling her long-term priorities. Jesus reminded Martha to pursue both lifelong commitment and daily service. **Read their story in Luke 10:38–42. What did Jesus teach them about priorities? Summarize His instructions here.**

Jesus spoke clearly yet lovingly when He said, *"Martha, Martha, you are worried and upset about many things, but one thing is necessary. Mary has made the right choice, and it will not be taken away from her"* (vv. 41–42). He continues to challenge His followers to pursue proper priorities with determination and discipline. Christians should choose what is lasting, a personal relationship with Jesus Christ.

Goals are essential for successful living. Someone once said that he who aims at nothing hits it every time. You will be unproductive without realistic goals. You will hit your target—nothing. It is very important to depend on God for guidance and power. While it has been said that accomplishments come by "aspiration, inspiration, and perspiration," as Christians we receive the desire, discipline, and determination from God. Consider the suggestions below as your set personal goals. The Lord has used these general guidelines to help me:

1. **Start simply.** Pick a fairly easy initial goal. Early success is a real encouragement.
2. **Be specific.** Don't set vague, undefined goals. You are more likely to accomplish clear, meaningful goals.
3. **Be realistic.** Try to identify goals within your reach. Break larger goals into smaller ones to ensure that they are attainable.
4. **Be decisive.** Once you decide to do something, do it! Indecision wastes a lot of time.
5. **Learn to say no.** When a task doesn't help you accomplish one of your goals, don't do it. Say no to others in a gentle but firm way.
6. **Check your progress regularly.** It is helpful to monitor your

progress periodically. If progress is minimal, you may need to redirect your goals.

7. **Revise your goals as needed.** There may be factors beyond your control that force you to reassess your goals. Be flexible when your initial plans must change.

8. **Reward your accomplishments.** Don't forget to praise yourself when you complete a goal. Positive rewards will keep you working.

My husband, Chuck, and I have developed a practice of evaluating and setting goals as each year ends and the new one begins. Sometimes during the week between Christmas and New Year's Day, he and I separately spend time reflecting on what we have accomplished with the help of the Lord during the past year. Then we set personal goals for the upcoming year. After the time of individual reflection, we share our goals with each other. It is wonderful to hear Chuck's goals for the future and to share mine. We are strengthened by the prayers and support of the other. Share your goals with someone once you have set them.

Identification of weaknesses and establishment of goals will help you personalize discipline. You must also reward your accomplishments to promote perseverance in personal discipline. Personal discipline is a process that can only be fulfilled with the help of God and others.

Reward Accomplishments

Rewards—this is my favorite part of personal discipline. I love to celebrate accomplishments and reward successes. God does too! He loves to bless His children for their faithfulness. He blesses obedient followers immediately and eternally. We enjoy rewards on earth and will experience them in heaven. So, seize the moment—reward your accomplishments.

The Lord faithfully rewards His children in the earthly realm. His blessings are immeasurable. Some of His blessings flow from His mercy—undeserved, unearned on our part. Other blessings are for righteous living and devoted service. God blesses His children with good health and long life. He blesses us with happy marriages and loving families. He blesses us with significant work and meaningful ministries. What a gracious and generous God!

As you consider the blessings of God, reflect on the rewards He has given you already. Who or what are some of your most treasured blessings? As you write them below, thank God for His many blessings.

_____

_____

God does immediately bestow blessings on His faithful children. He also promises eternal rewards for righteous living.

Scripture refers to "crowns," both literal and figurative. A crown may be an actual headdress worn by royalty (David's crown in 2 Samuel 12:30 or the high priest's crown in Leviticus 8:9). Most often the New Testament refers to a crown figuratively—a future reward for good behavior. **Read the following references and identify the specific crown awarded by the Lord. Fill in the blanks below.**

1 Corinthians 9:25 — an _____ _crown_
1 Thessalonians 2:19 — _a crown of_ _____
2 Timothy 4:8 — _a crown of_ _____
James 1:12 — _the crown of_ _____
1 Peter 5:4 — _the crown of_ _____

To those who follow God and accomplish His purpose, He gives rewards—heavenly crowns.

God promises rewards to those who live for Him. The crowns He bestows are _"imperishable"_—they never fade away (1 Corinthians 9:25). He gives a _"crown of rejoicing"_—abundant living forever (1 Thessalonians 2:19). He gives a _"crown of righteousness"_—a reward for godliness (2 Timothy 4:8). He gives the _"crown of life"_—eternity with God Himself (James 1:12). And He gives the _"crown of glory"_— the ultimate reward when the child of God becomes perfected in Him (1 Peter 5:4). The rewards from the Father are abundant and personalized. He selects for each child a reward appropriate for their efforts and satisfying of their desires. He wants to bless us as we bring honor to Him.

To His disciples, Jesus charged: *"If anyone wants to come with Me, he must deny himself, take up his cross daily, and follow Me"* (Luke 9:23). In the pursuit of discipline, we must decide to follow the Lord not only in salvation but in daily living. We must sacrifice our personal agendas and deny our selfish ambitions in order to seek His will and purpose. We are to follow Him daily, all the days of our lives. This is the Bible's prescription for personalized discipline.

What are the three D's in Luke 9:23 that will help develop divine discipline? Write them below.

> D_____
> D_____
> D_____

If you sincerely *desire* to follow Christ, you must *deny* yourself and follow Him *daily*. That is Jesus' own personalization of discipline. You will develop self-control if you follow this biblical plan.

I truly experienced God's plan for rewards as I pursued my doctorate. I had a strong desire to gain more education, to prepare for my career and calling. In order to achieve my goal and do well in graduate school, I had to deny myself of many things. Mostly I had to deny myself time to do the things I enjoyed, to be with others, or to simply relax or rest. That denial was difficult and painful at times. And, I had to renew my commitment to my studies and to the denial on a daily basis. But after a period of time, that discipline paid off. I achieved my goal and completed my degree. The rewards have been great. Not only have I experienced personal satisfaction, but my academic accomplishments have paved the way for career pursuits and ministry effectiveness. It was a tough journey but a rewarding one.

What a challenge! We must personalize discipline—practice control in our own lives. Have you begun the process? Have you identified your own weaknesses? Have you set realistic goals? And have you begun to enjoy some rewards for your accomplishments? If your answers are yes, then you can pray this prayer of commitment with me: *Lord, I will come after You. I will deny myself daily and follow You.* When you have verbalized this commitment and taken these steps, you have personalized discipline. Now you must *persevere* in the disciplined life—keep on!

My Personal Discipline

Since you have completed eight lessons in this study of self-control, take a few minutes to evaluate your personal progress. How well are you doing in your pursuit of divine discipline? Honestly answer the following questions yes or no, then explain.

Have you personalized discipline in your life? _____ How?

_____

_____

Have you identified your personal weaknesses? _____ What?

_____

_____

Have you set some goals for discipline? _____ What?

_____

_____

Have you experienced some rewards for your discipline? ___ What?

_____

_____

Dear Lord:
I have recognized my weaknesses, and I have set some personal goals.
Now I will enjoy Your rewards for my accomplishments. Amen.

Lesson 9
Perseverance in Discipline for a Lifetime

Divine Instruction

For this very reason, make every effort to supplement your faith with goodness, goodness with knowledge, knowledge with self-control, self-control with endurance, endurance with godliness, godliness with brotherly affection, and brotherly affection with love. —2 Peter 1:5–7

By now, you should be convinced of the importance of self-control and convicted of any lack of discipline in your own life. You have learned how to develop self-control in your life by adding God's supernatural power and people's persuasive power to your own personal willpower. Once you have personalized discipline in your life, you can begin to gain control of all areas of your life. Now it's time to learn the lesson that will help personal discipline last for a lifetime. The key to maintaining a disciplined life is **perseverance**.

The word *perseverance* is not commonly used in conversation or even casually considered in society today. In fact, the opposite is true. Since commitment is rarely practiced, inconsistency is widely accepted. People often start but don't continue personal disciplines. However, perseverance is a powerful word, often used in Scripture. It is a key concept in the pursuit of self-control. Let's try to better understand this biblical teaching.

In *Merriam-Webster's* dictionary, *perseverance* is defined as: "persistence in a state, enterprise, or undertaking in spite of counter influences, opposition, or discouragement." Opposition and discouragement are expected in the course of living. One must persevere in order to continue on. The *Holman Bible Dictionary* says that *perseverance* is "maintaining Christian faith through the trying times." An obedient Christian is expected faithfully to endure and to remain steadfast in the face of opposition, attack, and discouragement. What is your perseverance quotient? Are you able to stand firmly in the trials of life?

Perseverance is essential for success and happiness in life! It characterizes the individual who is determined, persistent, and stubborn. In order to accomplish goals, one must continue diligently along a definite course and remain focused in spite of obstacles. Stick with it! Don't give up! Hang in there! Don't let anything stop you! These attitudes are essential for perseverance.

I learned my greatest lesson in perseverance during my three-year pursuit of a doctorate. It was a challenging process, and I was often tempted to give up. But God taught me to persevere. Even when the labor was long, I persevered. I worked all day, attended class in the evening, studied at night, and wrote papers on the weekend. My perseverance made a permanent impact on my life. The same God who called me to pursue an advanced degree sustained me during my studies. I finished the course, accomplished my goal. But I also learned the invaluable lesson of perseverance. Many of my colleagues did not persevere, so they did not graduate. Some of the brightest didn't finish because they gave up. Chuck and I often say that a doctorate is not a measure of intelligence; it is an award for perseverance.

The Bible teaches us about perseverance. Scripture encourages us to be steadfast, to continue growing, and to remain faithful. We are to imitate Christ who is unfailing in His love, mercy, and grace. Many New Testament passages include perseverance as a godly trait of faithful Christians. Peter begins his second epistle with instructions in righteousness. He claims that perseverance and other Christlike virtues are to be added to our faith.

Read 2 Peter 1:5–11 to understand the importance of perseverance in the Christian's life. In the spaces below, write the specific traits to be added to faith.

Faith + _____

Faith + _____

Faith + _____

Faith + _____

Faith + _____

Faith + _____

Faith + _____

Every believer is to strengthen her faith in God by adding righteousness—"add to your faith *goodness*, to goodness *knowledge*, to knowledge *self-control*, to self-control *endurance*, to endurance *godliness*, to godliness *brotherly affection*, and to brotherly affection *love*." Only when you diligently pursue Christlikeness will you grow spiritually. Perseverance is a part of the growth process. It requires *patience*, demands *persistence*, and results in *permanence*.

Patience

Perseverance requires patience. Since trials in life are inevitable, Christians must learn to endure without complaint and bear suffering with peace. Patience is a virtue that many Christians do not possess! While some of us manage to endure, few of us endure without complaint. Jesus endured persecution and scorn without shame. Even though He possessed the power to defeat His enemies, Jesus was victorious as He persevered. He patiently suffered for our salvation.

In the Book of Hebrews, we are reminded to endure hardships, avoid sin, and persevere in life just as Jesus did:

> *"Therefore, since we also have such a large cloud of witnesses surrounding us, let us lay aside every weight and the sin that so easily ensnares us. Let us run with endurance the race that lies before us, keeping our eyes on Jesus, the source and perfecter of our faith, who for the joy that lay before Him endured a cross and despised the shame and has sat down at the right hand of God's throne"* (Hebrews 12:1–3).

Jesus, who also provided our salvation, modeled endurance. He also gives us patience in our suffering.

I am not always a patient person. While it is easier for me to be patient with other people, I am often impatient with myself.

Only months after our marriage, my dear husband observed my lack of patience. While cooking dinner, my inexpensive hand-mixer would not blend the mashed potatoes. It smoked and sputtered. I got *so* frustrated. In my frustration, I picked up the mixer, which promptly flung potatoes all over the kitchen. Chuck watched in disbelief as his exasperated wife lost control. I had no patience with myself or that mixer. (By the way, my concerned husband gave me a brand-new electric mixer for Christmas that year. He still likes to tell people that the mixer saved our marriage!)

Are you a patient person? Even if you are typically patient, there are probably times when you lose control. Try to remember a recent example of your impatience. Briefly summarize the experience in the space below.

_____

_____

As you recall your lack of patience, confess your sin and ask God to give you His power to endure.

The Apostle Paul practiced patience in his suffering and perseverance in his faith. He evidenced spiritual maturity and unending joy despite his circumstances. In Romans 5:3–4, Paul challenges us as believers to *"rejoice in our afflictions, because we know that affliction produces endurance, endurance produces proven character, and proven character produces hope."* Paul testifies of a faith that triumphed in trials. He acknowledges that his power to persevere was from God: *"God's love has been poured out in our hearts through the Holy Spirit who was given to us"* (Romans 5:5). The Holy Spirit will give you patience to persevere even when you have no patient for yourself.

Later in the New Testament, Christians are challenged to persevere with joy in the midst of trials. **Read James 1:2–4 to understand the benefit of trials. What does the Bible teach about trials?**

How should you respond to trials?_____

_____

When do you face trials? _____

_____

Why do you experience trials? _____

_____

What do you learn from trials? _____

_____

Though it is not easy, Christians should respond to trials with joy, knowing that God is in control.

Trials are an inevitable part of life, coming when we least expect them. Trials can produce patience in the life of a persevering saint. And trials perfect and complete the Christian. This passage in James reinforces the fact that God helps the faithful to persevere. James 1:5 says: *"Now if any of you lacks wisdom, he should ask God, who gives to all generously and without criticizing, and it will be given to him."* The Lord is the source of our patience, and He gives it generously and without chiding.

As Christians, our secret of a joyful life is our confidence that God will overcome if we persevere. We must discipline ourselves with patience to endure life's challenges. A part of perseverance is also persistence—continued endurance, not just momentary discipline.

Persistence

Perseverance demands persistence. God wants His children to be patient in enduring hardships and persistent in pursuing objectives. God desires for us to be clear in purpose and focused on personal goals. Paul encouraged fellow Christians to be tenacious—to persist in their goals in order to win the prize. Written in a time when athletics was a focus of society, Paul used the imagery of a track event to describe his own race.

Not that I have already reached the goal or am already fully mature, but I make every effort to take hold of it because I also have been

taken hold of by Christ Jesus. Brothers, I do not consider myself to have taken hold of it. But one thing I do: forgetting what is behind and reaching forward to what is ahead, I pursue as my goal the prize promised by God's heavenly call in Christ Jesus.
—Philippians 3:12–14

Paul the Apostle sought to be steadfast. We, too, should persist in our purpose—to know God and to walk in His power.

Are you persistent in your faith? Have you continued to grow in the Lord or has your spiritual life wavered? **Can you recall times in your life when your faith has not been strong? When has your faith been weak? Note here a time when you did not persist.**

_____

_____

Some years ago I faced some health challenges and my faith wavered. When I felt bad or had little energy, I became discouraged. It was easy for me to lose hope. I could not imagine how the woman with a hemorrhage persisted as the years passed. When I recognized my own weakness, I turned to God for His strength. He gave me patience to continue even when I was tired. He helped me persist even when I didn't feel well. My physical condition taught me perseverance, total dependence on Him for strength and comfort. He can give that same power to you.

Persistence in faith is a source of personal strength and a witness in the world. A friend of mine recently made a comment that illustrates the impact of a persistent faith. He said, "I am much more impressed with the testimony of a person who has always walked with the Lord than a person who after rebellion returns to the Lord." Consistency in the Christian life is a powerful testimony. While a dramatic conversion experience may get attention, a persistent faith will keep the attention of the world.

A young woman we know had a brain hemorrhage at age 24. Although she survived, she was left severely impaired by the stroke. She has worked to regain her abilities to eat, walk, talk, and be independent. It has been a long, hard road. But, she has been strong in her faith and has persisted in therapy. Her husband and family have supported her and have never given up. She has improved significantly though she has a long way to go. And, she has been a powerful witness in the world as her faith has sustained her. She recently proclaimed the next year in her journey as her "year of hope." Her patience and persistence in the face of struggle has not only strengthened her faith but has strengthened us all!

The Book of Revelation affirms the persistence of believers in the early church. Seven churches in Revelation are identified and several of them are praised for faithfulness. **Read the commendation for these churches in the passages below. Determine what behavior is rewarded.**

Revelation 2: 2–3 (Ephesus) = _____

Revelation 2:19 (Thyatira) = _____

Revelation 3:10 (Philadelphia) = _____

John commended three of the seven churches in Revelation for their perseverance. Although they had other big problems, John recognized that they persisted in their faith, in obedience, and in service. They endured their challenges with patience.

The church in Ephesus was affirmed because of "works, your labor, and your endurance." They persevered for the sake of the Lord (Revelation 2:2–3). The church in Thyatira was commended for its works, love, service, faith, and patience. Their recent works had been greater than their first (Revelation 2:19). The church in Philadelphia was also praised for obedience and patience. God promised to spare them the wrath on the world (Revelation 3:10). Those Christians in the early church learned perseverance as they persisted in their faith. God will bless all of His children who continue to follow Him.

In his letter to the Romans, Paul reminded his fellow Christians to help others persist in their faith. Spiritual strength in one can enrich others and bring glory to God. This truth is found in Romans 15:4–6:

For whatever was written in the past was written for our instruction, so that we may have hope through endurance and through the encouragement from the Scriptures. Now may the God who gives endurance and encouragement allow you to live in harmony with one another, according to the command of Christ Jesus, so that you may glorify the God and Father of our Lord Jesus Christ with a united mind and voice.
—Romans 15:4–6

God, who is patient, teaches us patience so that we might persevere in faith and stimulate others to persist in faith even in the midst of trials. Our perseverance brings glory to God. If you continue to grow in the Lord and serve Him, your disciplined lifestyle will also become permanent.

Permanence

Perseverance results in permanence. Though at first discipline is painful and uncomfortable, it becomes less painful and more comfortable as it is practiced. Discipline comes more naturally as it becomes a permanent part of daily life. Christians must always love God, trust God, and serve God. We should be faithful always, like He is faithful always (Matthew 28:20).

An attitude or behavior becomes permanent when you always think it or do it. The Bible gives specific instructions about permanent living—those "always behaviors." **Read the following Scriptures and identify those actions that should always be a part of the Christian's life.**

Luke 18:1 _____

John 18:20 _____

1 Corinthians 1:4 _____

2 Corinthians 5:6 _____

Philippians 1:20 _____

Colossians 4:12 _____

1 Peter 3:15 _____

Jesus told His children to pray always, to be constantly in conversation with Him (Luke 18:1). He told us to always teach the truth and always give thanks to God (John 18:20, 2 Corinthians 1:4). The Christian should always be confident in the Lord and always be bold in witnessing to others (2 Corinthians 5:6, Philippians 1:20). We should always work fervently for the Lord and always be ready to defend our faith (Colossians 4:12, 1 Peter 3:15). Permanence is a recurring theme in the Bible because the Lord wants His children to consistently live for Him.

In his first letter to the Christians in Thessalonica, Paul concluded with several exhortations. He challenged them to always rejoice, always pray, and always give thanks:

> *Rejoice always!*
> *Pray constantly.*
> *Give thanks in everything,*
> *for this is God's will for you in Christ Jesus*
> —1 Thessalonians 5:16–18

The Lord calls all His children to a life of permanence—always live in faith.

Spiritual discipline and personal discipline must become a permanent part of your life. Your commitments must last for a lifetime. I have more trouble continuing my physical commitments than my spiritual ones. I can maintain discipline in my Bible study, prayer, and service because I know that pleases God. But I often struggle with my physical discipline. It is hard to eat properly when I love food and entertain often. It is difficult to exercise regularly when my schedule is so busy. I do know that God wants me to be consistent in all my disciplines—spiritual and physical.

Most of us who have struggled with a weight problem realize that a diet is successful only if permanent changes are made. A lifestyle of healthy eating must be developed. Every effective diet plan includes a maintenance program. The National Center for Health

Statistics reports that the rate of regain on any weight-loss regime is 95 percent unless permanent changes in eating and exercise are made. The failure rate is high because most dieters do not persevere—they make few permanent lifestyle changes.

In which areas of your life do you falter? Are there certain behaviors that you should maintain permanently in your life? Why is permanence in desired behaviors important to you?

You probably understand the importance of permanence in discipline, but you can't seem to stick with it. Don't be discouraged by your failure.

Because perseverance isn't a natural behavior, we will all experience setbacks. It is more common for people to fail in their attempts than to succeed. You see, *lapses are the rule rather than the exception*. We must train ourselves to put failures behind and move on toward success. In their book, *The New Aerobics for Women*, Kenneth and Millie Cooper discuss the psychological motivators that keep people exercising. They encourage us to persevere—to make exercise a permanent lifestyle. They encourage us to "perceive a lapse as a momentary interruption; do not see it as a failure forever. Forgive yourself and start again, whether it's for the second time or the twentieth." That's good advice for persevering in physical and spiritual discipline.

Charles Swindoll supports a similar viewpoint in his book, *Starting Over*. He concurs that success is not measured as much by the absence of failure as by the willingness to start over. Swindoll states, "The person who succeeds is not the one who holds back, fearing failure, nor the one who never fails...but rather the one who moves on in spite of failure." God still wants to use us even when we stumble, but He can't if we refuse to get up. We must persevere throughout our lifetimes.

It is a great consolation to know that God forgives us when we fail, and He helps us start over again. The prophet Jonah learned that lesson when God gave him a second chance to go to Nineveh.

At first Jonah tried to run away from God. After God punished him with three days in the belly of a great fish, Jonah cried out to God. Jonah 3:1 says that *"Then the word of the LORD came to Jonah a second time."* The reluctant prophet was given a second chance, and he spoke God's word of warning in Nineveh. God will work through us if we will start again. Our God is the God of second chances! He also wants His children to continue in their faith without wavering.

My dad is a modern testimony that God gives His children a second chance. When my dad left the Lord, the Lord never left him. He never stopped seeking His lost sheep. After years of running from the Lord, God convicted my dad of his sin and forgave him. He was restored to a new relationship with Christ. God gave my dad a second chance like Jonah and so many of His rebellious children. Only when we persevere and persist in godliness will we resist rebellion and experience permanent life change.

As Christians, we must keep growing. We must persevere in godly living. If we develop and maintain godly virtues daily, they will become habits—good habits. The more we practice spiritual disciplines, the more disciplined we become. Good habits need to be permanent.

God wants His children to persevere in godliness, to develop and maintain spiritual disciplines. In my book *Divine Discipline*, I created an acrostic to reinforce the importance of perseverance. I hope this sequence of words will help you remember how to continue in the faith.

Persistence
Endurance
Renewal
Steadfastness
Excellences
Vitality
Effort
Recommitment
Enthusiasm

These descriptions of discipline are intended to help you persevere in personal discipline. In the process of divine discipline, perseverance is the determiner of long-term success. If you learn *patience* and *persistence*, your perseverance can become *permanent*. God, who is always available, wants to empower you for a life of personal discipline.

My Personal Discipline

Read the following Scripture aloud as a commitment to your perseverance in faith. Underline key words and phrases to remember.

Therefore, my dear brothers, be steadfast, immovable, always excelling in the Lord's work, knowing that your labor in the Lord is not in vain.
—1 Corinthians 15:58

Though perseverance in the faith is at times difficult, the Lord will reward your discipline.

Dear Lord:
It is so hard to stay disciplined. Please help me to be patient when facing hardships and to be persistent in life's challenges so my discipline will result in truly permanent lifetime changes. Amen.

Lesson 10
Self-Control and the Rewards of Discipline

Divine Instruction

Everyone who competes exercises self-control in everything. However, they do it to receive a crown that will fade away, but we a crown that will never fade away. — 1 Corinthians 9:25

The promises of God are great! While we cannot always depend on the commitment of others, the promises of God are trustworthy. His promises are never broken and they are eternal. The Bible is filled with precious promises from God to His children. Bible scholars have identified more than 30,000 promises in God's Word—promises of protection, comfort, guidance, forgiveness, and love. The precious promises of God can be claimed by anyone who trusts Him for salvation and follows Him in godly living. Scripture clearly affirms that God has *"given us very great and precious promises, so that through them you may share in the divine nature, escaping the corruption that is in the world because of evil desires"* (2 Peter 1:4).

What is a promise? A promise is the pledge of one person to another to fulfill a specific act. God makes many pledges to His children—promises to work in their lives. His promises are always fulfilled.

God's promises are dependable and they are generously bestowed. We do not receive blessings from God because of our merit. He promises to bless us because He is merciful and loving. The promises of God are not a result of our works but His grace. God promises to reward His children who faithfully live a disciplined life.

Take a few moments to reflect on the promises of God, which are offered to you. **List below at least ten of those precious promises. As you write them, voice a prayer of gratitude to your gracious God. God promises me:**

1. _____

2. _____

3. _____

4. _____

5. _____

6. _____

7. _____

8. _____

9. _____

10. _____

The Bible records many promises of God. He made covenants with individuals like Abraham and David (Genesis 12:7, 2 Samuel 7:9). He made promises to nations like Israel (Genesis 22:18). And God made promises of a Messiah (Isaiah 9:6–7). The promises of the Old Testament were fulfilled in the New Testament. The promises of the New Testament are being fulfilled today. The old covenant was revealed in Jesus Christ, who provides salvation and freedom from the law (Romans 7:4).

Are you enjoying the promises of God? If not, you may wonder why. In order to receive God's promises, a person must first repent of sins, then follow in faith, and persevere in obedience. The Bible includes several conditional promises made by God to His children. While God is the giver of all blessings, each believer must bear some responsibility. These are not promises with strings attached, but agreements requiring action. The Lord Himself said, *"If My people who are called by My name humble themselves, pray and seek My face, and turn from their evil ways, then I will hear from heaven, forgive their sin and heal their land"* (2 Chronicles 7:14). If we Christians turn to God, repent of our sins, and live godly lives, then God promises to hear our prayers, forgive our sins, and restore our lives. It is an "if-then" promise.

As a child growing up, I received many promises from my parents. They promised to take care of me and provide me with an education. Those promises were based on their love for me not my efforts or merit. However, they also promised to pay me an allowance if I did my chores. That promise was conditional, if-then. My allowance was based upon my actions. So, like the Lord, people make promises. Some are unconditional and some are conditional. We learn to trust those who make promises to us and respond to them in gratitude. The unconditional promises are ours because of love. The conditional promises are ours because of obedience.

In this lesson we will explore the promises or rewards given by God to His children who follow in obedience. There are many rewards of self-discipline! Rewards are experienced here on earth and later for all eternity in heaven. While our motivation for self-control in our daily lives should not be recognition from God, our discipline is rewarded by His blessings. His rewards include *past blessing, present freedom,* and *future hope.* Let the promises of God give you courage and strength to persevere in personal discipline.

Past Blessing

Has God blessed your life? Most Christians feel we have been blessed beyond what we deserve. God has truly blessed me. His blessings in my life are immeasurable. He has given me a precious husband, a loving family, supportive friends, and meaningful ministry, not to mention the abundant provision of food, clothing, and shelter. He is such a generous God! As I reflect on my own life, I am overwhelmed with gratitude to God for all that He has done for me. Though I am undeserving of His blessings, I am grateful for His many kindnesses. Are you grateful for God's past blessing in your life?

Take a few moments and reflect back on the blessings of the Lord in your life. List below some of the past blessings for which you are grateful.

_____

_____

_____

My tendency at times is to reflect back to distant blessings, thanking God for my salvation as a child or the education of my youth. It is good to remember early blessings in your life. But God has also bestowed recent blessings on my life. He has strengthened me during surgery, protected my travels, and opened doors of ministry. Past blessings cover the years. He is an active God—at work in our lives continually. We should constantly praise Him for His blessings.

The psalmist David often praised God for His many blessings. **Read just one psalm of praise to develop an attitude of gratitude. As you read Psalm 103:1–5, fill in the blanks below.**

> *Bless the Lord, O my soul;*
> *And all that is within me, bless His holy name!*
> *Bless the Lord, O my soul,*
> *And forget not all His benefits:*
> *Who _____ all your iniquities,*
> *Who _____ all your diseases,*
> *Who _____ your life from destruction,*
> *Who _____ you with lovingkindness and tender mercies,*
> *Who _____ your mouth with good things,*
> *So that your youth is renewed like the eagle's.*
> —Psalm 103:1–5 (NKJV)

Why should we praise the Lord? Praise should be our response to our loving Father for His many blessings. He forgives, He heals, He redeems, He crowns, and He satisfies. And that is just a beginning of His bestowing of blessings on our lives. Nothing else can satisfy the soul like a close, personal relationship with the Lord.

God's blessings come to us in many different shapes and forms. Because God knows each of us intimately, He tailor-makes our personal blessings. However, the clearest image in the Bible of God's blessings for His children is found in the description of the fruit of the Spirit. Let's again consider these blessings of godly living—love, joy, peace, patience, kindness, goodness, faith, gentleness, and self-control. Self-control is essential in developing the fruit of the Spirit. And the fruit of the Spirit results from a disciplined life. Hebrews 12:11 promises *"a harvest of righteousness and peace for those who have been trained by it [discipline]"* (NIV). Persistence in spiritual discipline produces a fruitful life.

In the next few minutes, we will briefly examine each fruit of the Spirit to better understand God's blessings. This fruit inspection will focus on those rewards for discipline in relation to God, to others, and to self.

First, disciplined, godly living will be rewarded by the fruit of the Spirit as you relate to God—love, joy, and peace. Briefly define each word below.

Love _____

Joy _____

Peace _____

Love is unselfish, loyal, benevolent concern for the well-being of others. It is only possible as a result of discipline and is the greatest gift of all (1 Corinthians 13:13). *Joy* is true happiness and delight that overcomes natural feelings. As a result of self-discipline, a believer can experience true joy despite circumstances. *Peace* is the condition of well-being and tranquility. This reward of personal discipline comes from God as a result of obedience. These blessings are yours as you develop divine discipline.

Godly living will also be rewarded by the fruit of the Spirit as you relate to others—longsuffering (patience), kindness, and goodness. Briefly define each word below.

Patience _____

Kindness _____

Goodness _____

Patience or longsuffering is endurance in the face of adversity. God rewards His children with patience as we continue on in the faith when confronting challenges. *Kindness* is steadfast love expressed in action. Without personal discipline it is hard to be caring toward difficult people. *Goodness* is revealed in what we say and do. Generosity to others in words and actions is a grace gift of God. These blessings are also yours as you live out divine discipline.

Finally, godly living will be rewarded by the fruit of the Spirit as you relate to self—faith, gentleness, and self-control. Briefly define these words.

Faith _____

Gentleness _____

Self-control _____

Faith is personal loyalty and trustworthiness. Discipline leads to steadfast trust in God and commitment to others. *Gentleness* is a humble, sweet spirit, which comes only from God. It develops in the heart and is reflected in character. *Self-control* is the crowning fruit of the Spirit, the necessary ingredient to experience the blessings of God.

In Galatians 5, Paul pictures a beautiful tree bearing nine precious fruits. You will enjoy the fruit only when you diligently tend the tree. The tree of your life needs daily watering and continual pruning if it is to grow and flourish. Without personal discipline, you will not enjoy a *"harvest of righteousness and peace."* God's promised harvest has brought you *past blessings*, it is bringing you *present freedom*, and will bring you *future hope*.

Present Freedom

The word *discipline* rarely conjures up the notion of freedom. When considering personal discipline, it is natural to think of bondage and suffering. However, discipline is not a "bad word." The ultimate result of discipline is freedom. The disciplined personal life yields freedom in Christ for the believer. If you practice self-control, you no longer experience bondage to people or things. Your temporary sacrifice results in permanent freedom. The commitment of your heart frees you from the restriction of rules!

What responsibilities seem to tie you down? What demands in your life always consume your time? List those duties below that are presently filling your days.

Like most women, I wear many hats and juggle many balls. I have many different responsibilities. Right now, my time is filled with teaching classes, writing assignments, family concerns, and travel. My days are full and my nights are short. At busy times like this, I must be more disciplined than ever. If I will be determined to accomplish my goals and complete my tasks efficiently, I can actually have time to relax. I enjoy reading a magazine, taking a bubble bath, or talking with friends. Discipline in my work results in freedom—some time for myself. My schedule no longer holds me captive; I can enjoy the rewards of discipline—recognition of my achievements and time for personal reward.

What rewards do you enjoy as a result of getting your work done? **What relaxing activities do you enjoy most? Write them here then plan time to pamper yourself.**

What?	When?

Freedom is a treasure we seek. Everyone enjoys time for relaxation and relief of responsibilities. God created us to work, but He also created us to rest. God Himself modeled the rhythm of life in the process of creation. He worked the first six days and rested on the seventh. After creating the heavens and the earth, day and night, fish in the sea and birds in the air, male and female, He rested. Genesis 2:1–3 records God's plan for work and play.

> *So the heavens and the earth and everything in them were completed. By the seventh day God completed His work that He had done, and He rested on the seventh day from all His work that He had done. God blessed the seventh day and declared it holy, doe on it He rested from His work of creation.*
> —Genesis 2:1–3

What does this Scripture teach you about rest? Why is rest a freedom resulting from discipline?

_____

_____

Rest is but one freedom that results from discipline. Let's see what other freedoms can be experienced as we live a disciplined life.

The Bible teaches about freedom. Freedom is at the very core of the gospel and godly living. Galatians 5:1 informs believers that we are to *"stand fast in the liberty by which Christ Jesus has made us free"* (NKJV). Jesus provided freedom from the penalty of sin in His death on the cross. He provides freedom for us to live abundantly, and He offers freedom for all eternity. God has called *all* believers to freedom; His call is universal: *"For you were called to be free, brothers; only don't use this freedom as an opportunity for the flesh, but serve one another through love"* (Galatians 5:13). Freedom is not a license to disobey; it is freedom to obey God and serve others in love.

In his commentary on Galatians, John MacArthur discusses these four purposes of freedom. God gives us freedom: (1) to oppose the flesh, (2) to serve others, (3) to fulfill God's moral law, and (4) to avoid harming others. Self-control is necessary to experience these freedoms. Without divine discipline, we will be unable to resist sin, serve our fellowman, obey God's law, and love others. It is discipline that makes way for freedom.

Americans are blessed with the freedom to live our dreams, worship our God, and provide for our families. Many people of the world do not enjoy this freedom. They live in poverty and oppression. Many of them desire more than anything to come to America. They sacrifice their lives and possessions in the pursuit of freedom. Once here, they often struggle with the language and the culture as well as making a living for themselves and their families. However, most immigrants are grateful to be in a land of opportunity. They cherish their freedom. I have a friend from India who recently became a US citizen. She has truly fulfilled her life's dream for freedom. A Vietnamese owner of a small business in New Orleans was standing outside of his shop looking at the sign with his name on it. He shared with me his pride in finally achieving the means to provide for his family. Too often we take our freedom as Americans for granted. And too often we take our freedom as Christians for granted. Be grateful for the freedom you have in Christ.

Aren't you glad you don't have to earn freedom? Freedom is a gift from God, a result of your godly living. Richard Foster briefly mentions the reward of freedom in his book, *Celebration of Discipline*. He says, "Every discipline has its corresponding freedom, and the purpose of the disciplines is freedom." It is true that most of us seek freedom at any cost. Unfortunately, we are not often willing to pay the price of discipline to obtain freedom. Our goal is divine discipline. Our reward is freedom.

In his letter to the Romans, Paul explains freedom in the Lord. He writes that as believers we have been set free from sin and have become slaves of God (Romans 6:22). Our freedom from God requires our obedience. Divine discipline has been rewarded with *past blessing* and *present freedom*. God also promises us eternal life — out *future hope*.

Future Hope

Because I am somewhat impatient, I am grateful that God gives us immediate rewards for self-discipline. I am excited about crowns in glory, but I love blessings here on earth! It would be hard for me to patiently wait for God to recognize my discipline. Our past blessings and present freedom are magnified by our future hope.

How can we receive rewards in heaven? To whom does God present eternal rewards? According to Scripture, there are some specific criteria. Those who live in the flesh will not receive heavenly rewards. Those who live in the Spirit will reap an eternal harvest. The Bible teaches that there are only two fields in which seed can be sown—the field of the flesh or the field of the spirit. **Read Galatians 6:8-9 and summarize what the Bible saws about future rewards. Record your summary below.**

Scripture is clear. A sinful Christian reaps a harvest of pain and suffering now and no rewards in eternity. Sinful seeds produce empty rewards. The kind of harvest is determined by where and how the seed is planted. Some people plant seeds of the flesh—selfish, uncontrolled, human living. Life in the flesh reaps corruption and death. Others plant seeds of the Spirit—unselfish, disciplined, godly living. Life in the Spirit reaps joy and eternal life. Your future harvest is measured by where your present crop is planted. Disciplined living definitely has its rewards!

While a believer who "sows to her own flesh" does not lose her salvation, that believer certainly loses the fruit of the Spirit. Unrighteous Christians do not enjoy abundant living while on earth. It is sad to see Christians lose the joy of their salvation. King David knew what it was like to lose the joy of his salvation. Sin separated him from God and stopped the harvest of fruit in his life. In Psalm 51, he cried out to God: *"Restore the joy of Your salvation to me, and give me a willing spirit"* (v. 12). A sinful life produces temporary pleasures, but not eternal joy. Remain faithful to the Lord and enjoy His blessings now and in the future.

Faithfulness in godly living is rewarded by abundant blessings now and for eternity. Paul, the faithful apostle, reaped the fruit of the Spirit in this in this life. He testified, *"For who is our hope or joy or crown of boasting in the presence of our Lord Jesus at His coming? Is it not you?"* (1 Thessalonians 2:19). Paul was grateful for his rewards and reminded other Christians of their earlthly rewards for righteous living. Paul also reaped the rewards for devoted service in eternal life. He proclaimed God's promise: *"There is reserved for me in the future the crown of righteousness"* (2 Timothy 4:8). Right now Paul is wearing his crown in glory. Present blessings and future rewards are promised to all believers who persevere in disciplined living.

The Bible speaks of heavenly crowns. While we may think of crowns as royal headdresses, spiritual crowns are different. Royalty today wears crowns only for official ceremonies. How magnificent are the jeweled crowns! I was amazed when I viewed the crown jewels in London. The display of the royal jewelry of Britain was breathtaking. The crowns were filled with large diamonds and other precious gems. They sparkled and glittered beautifully.

Later I was even more amazed at the crown jewels of Turkey. The royal jewelry of the Sultans, displayed in their palace in Istanbul, was magnificent. It is hard to comprehend such wealth and opulence. But even those exquisite crowns tarnish and lose their luster. God's crowns are not fleeting wonders; they are eternal rewards.

What does the Bible mean when it mentions the "crown" given to believers? Write your definition here.

_____

_____

While the *Merriam-Webster* dictionary defines a *crown* as a royal headdress, it also describes a crown as a trophy: "a reward of victory or a mark of honor." Even the world recognizes the rewards of hard work. When Scripture speaks of crowns, it refers to additional rewards for Christian service given out in heaven. Several different types of crowns are mentioned in the Bible.

Read the following passages and identify the particular crown for believers. Explain why each is given.

James 1:12 — the crown of: _____ **Why?**

_____

1 Thessalonians 2:19 — the crown of: _____ Why

_____

2 Timothy 4:8 — the crown of: _____ Why?

_____

1 Peter 5:4 — the crown of: _____ Why?

_____

James 1:12 discusses the *crown of life* — a prize of kingly glory worn by Christians who persevered in their faith through trials. The *crown of rejoicing* is described in 1 Thessalonians 2:19. It is given to Christians who keep the Word of God even in the face of persecution. The third reference, 2 Timothy 4:8, mentions a *crown of righteousness* given for godly living and dedicated service. The last heavenly crown is found in 1 Peter 5:4. An eternal *crown of glory* awaits all Christian leaders or under-shepherds who feed their flock according to the will of God. These heavenly crowns give future hope!

Later in the New Testament, Paul describes a lasting crown: *"we receive a crown that will never fade away"* (1 Corinthians 9:25). While athletes who train for competition win a perishable crown or crowns that will vanish, the Christian who practices discipline receives a crown that will last forever. While we can enjoy the memory of past blessings and the joy of present freedom, we can anticipate our future hope — rewards in heaven.

In my Granddaddy Harrington's last days, he loved to talk about heaven. A retired Methodist minister, he recited favorite Bible promises. He looked forward to being in the presence of God and the reunion with his beloved wife and precious mother. During a visit with him, Granddaddy asked me to read Revelation 4 and 5. As I read those verses aloud, I was reminded of our future hope.

"After this I looked, and there in heaven was an open door. The first voice that I heard speaking to me like a trumpet said, 'Come up here, and I will show you what must take place after this. Immediately I was in the Spirit, and a throne was set there in heaven. One was seated on the throne.'"
—Revelation 4:1–2

As my dad is aging, he loves to talk about the rewards in heaven he will receive because of his soul winning. During his life and ministry, he has won many people to faith in Jesus. Dad often tells people that the Bible calls the soul winner wise (Proverbs 11:30). My dad believes he has been cared for by the Lord and will continue to receive the blessings of the Lord because he has been a faithful witness. In fact, my dad would like his tombstone to say: "Bob Harrington, Certified Soul Winner." All Christians are promised rewards in heaven. But, those who have led others to faith in Christ will receive many crowns in glory.

God gives us such precious rewards here on earth and for all eternity! His rewards are past, present, and future. What a generous God!

My Personal Discipline

Read the following passages from Proverbs. What does each one teach about God's promises for disciplined living? Write a short answer in the space provided.

Proverbs 10:6 _____

Proverbs 10:25 _____

Proverbs 10:28 _____

Proverbs 11:8 _____

Proverbs 11:30 _____

Thank God for His precious promises!

Dear Lord:
Thank You for the rewards of a disciplined life—the past blessing, the present freedom, and the future hope. You are a trustworthy God! Amen.

Lesson 11
Self-Control and Other Disciplines

Divine Instruction

Discipline yourself for the purpose of godliness; for bodily discipline is only of little profit, but godliness is profitable for all things, since it holds promise for the present life and also for the life to come.
—1 Timothy 4:7–8 (NASB)

Nothing is more heartbreaking than something that fails to grow or someone who never reaches full potential. A seedling that never matures into a beautiful plant or majestic tree is disappointing. An intelligent, gifted person who lacks initiative is tragic. Many of us have special abilities that we never develop. Our lack of self-determination limits our personal growth and spiritual maturity. Healthy growth requires discipline in every area of life.

Many Christians demonstrate physical and mental growth without signs of spiritual maturity. They remain *"babes in Christ"* (1 Peter 2:1–3). New believers often remain immature because they fail to grow in their faith. Lack of personal discipline is life-limiting. The Lord wants us to grow in every aspect of life. Jesus Himself grew "in wisdom and stature, and in favor with God and with people" (Luke 2:52). Christians need to develop in all areas of life and in proper balance. Equal discipline and proportionate growth in every area of life is God's plan.

Balance in discipline is the key! It is natural for every believer to be stronger in one area of life and weaker in others. But discipline in every life realm is essential to healthy growth. **What is meant by the word *balance*? Write your understanding of this term in the space provided.**

_____

_____

Balance implies equal proportion among all parts. With proper distribution, equilibrium or balance is maintained. *Merriam-Webster's* dictionary defines *balance* as, "a state of harmony or proportion." When one dimension of life is undeveloped, life becomes out of balance. God desires His children to have a balanced, healthy life. God can make balance possible.

In *Women Reaching Women*, Chris Adams relates Monte Clendinning's ideas about balance in ministry: Many of the principles for Christian service also apply to personal life. A person needs balance of the mind, heart, and will—intellect, emotions, and actions. Balance can be achieved through discipline in all areas: spiritual, relational, physical, emotional, and mental. When even one aspect of life is undisciplined, the person is unbalanced or out of sync.

In the space provided below, draw a circle then divide it into parts to represent the different areas of your life. Try to reflect the accurate proportion of your time and energies invested in each area.

It is hard to accurately reflect personal priorities because life is constantly changing. But the goal of the Christian's life should be disciplined growth in essential areas. Mrs. Clendinning suggests that balance "can be maintained through regular evaluation, sensitive observation, and an outsider's perspective." The spiritual element of balance is God's work. His power is available to help us live a balanced life.

Some years ago, God taught Chuck and me a powerful lesson about balance in our priorities. As we were teaching Philippians 3:12–14, God's purpose became clear. Christians are to do *one thing* and that is *know Christ*. Instead of listing our life priorities in order from one to ten, we now focus our priorities around Christ, knowing and following Him. We draw a wheel with Christ as the center or hub and our priorities as the spokes around the wheel. It is amazing how life maintains balance when we keep Christ at the center. Our lives also get off balance when He is not the central focus.

Turn in your Bible to Philippians 3:12–14. Read the passage then summarize it in your own words below.

Paul learned about balance as he tried to manage his busy life and ministry. Though he had accomplished many things for Christ, he had not achieved his ultimate goal of knowing Christ fully. He forgot the past and reached ahead to the future. He knew nothing else mattered but his relationship with Christ.

Paul first discussed this priority in Philippians 3:8-10: *"I also consider everything to be a loss in view of the surpassing value of knowing Christ Jesus my Lord...so that I may gain Christ and be found in Him, not having a righteousness of my own from the law, but one that is through faith in Christ—the righteousness from God based on faith. My goal is to know Him and the power of His resurrection and the fellowship of His sufferings."* What an important priority! What a key to balance!

In this lesson, we will study the disciplines of life from three perspectives—spiritual, personal, and mental. As you study God's Word and receive His power, you will be better able to practice discipline. The good news is that discipline is not for spiritual giants only. All Christians can practice divine discipline to promote maturity and produce God's pleasure. Let's do some personal evaluation and make practical application of biblical instruction.

Spiritual Discipline

For the Christian, spiritual growth is expected. A Christian should not only accept Jesus Christ as personal Savior but should also follow Him as Lord. Spiritual growth depends upon discipline. In his work, *Spiritual Disciplines for the Christian Life*, Don Whitney discusses specific habits of spiritual maturity. He includes a thorough examination of Bible study, prayer, worship, evangelism, service, stewardship, fasting, silence and solitude journaling, and learning. Other sources include additional topics such as personal purity, simplicity, confession, celebration, sacrifice, and affirmation as spiritual disciplines. Don Whitney concludes that "spiritual disciplines are the God-given means we are to use in the Spirit–filled pursuit of godliness."

In this section we will take time to consider only Bible study, prayer, and witnessing. You should explore other spiritual disciplines as a follow-up study. First, let's talk about the study of God's Word. *Bible study* is essential for spiritual growth. What food is to physical life, God's Word is to spiritual life. **Remind yourself why Bible study is necessary for your spiritual growth. Read the Scriptures below and identify the Bible's work in your life.**

John 5:39 _____

Psalm 119: 9–11 _____

Proverbs 3:5–6 _____

2 Timothy 3:16–17 _____

Acts 22:14–15 _____

The Bible reveals to us who God is (John 5:39) and makes us aware of sin (Psalm 119:9–11). The Bible guides us and directs us throughout life (Proverbs 3:5–6). The Bible helps us live the godly life of a disciple (2 Timothy 3:16–17) and empowers us in evangelism (Acts 22:14–15). If we fail to study the Bible personally, we will not grow spiritually. If we discipline ourselves to faithfully study His Word, we will gain spiritual maturity. The writer of Hebrews describes the levels of spiritual life:

> *Although by this time you ought to be teachers, you need someone to teach you again the basic principles of God's revelation again. You need milk not solid food. Now everyone who lives on milk is*

inexperienced with the message about righteousness, because he is an infant. But solid food is for the mature—for those whose senses have been trained to distinguish between good and evil.
—Hebrews 5:12–14

We will be considered mature when we have our "senses to distinguish between good and evil." Intensive, personal Bible study is necessary for spiritual growth.

To maintain consistency in your Bible study, you must set aside a time and place for it. You should also collect Bible resources to enrich your personal study. There are so many excellent Bible studies available for individual use or group participation. Many Bible study tools are produced to assist with personal study. Be sure to have a Bible dictionary, a general commentary, and a Bible atlas in your own library for additional reference.

A Christian's greatest enemy of Bible study is time. There never seems to be enough time in the day for the study of God's Word. I struggle personally with discipline in my Bible study. It is difficult to find time to read the Scriptures I must teach, much less study the Scriptures I must learn. Discipline is required for my systematic personal study of God's Word.

What was the last passage of Scripture you read? What did it teach you? Write your insights here and meditate on the meaning.

_____

_____

Prayer is another important spiritual discipline. A Christian matures as she communicates with God. Oswald Chambers once said, "It is not so true that 'prayer changes things' as that prayer changes me and I change things." A disciplined prayer life changes the heart and soul of the believer. In prayer, God reveals Himself and His will as well as provides guidance for life. The undisciplined Christian misses out on fellowship with the Father. (See Jude 20, 21 and Jeremiah 9:23–24.)

Jude urged Christians to build up their faith and pray in the Holy Spirit. He recognized that they could not grow or remain steadfast without spending time in prayer. The prophet Jeremiah also understood that wise men could only boast in the Lord if they knew Him and spent time with Him. God truly delights in His children who commune with Him in prayer.

I have found these practical procedures to be helpful in disciplining my prayer life. You may benefit from them too.

- Set a definite time and place for prayer.
- Select some prayer resources (Bible, prayer journal, devotional book, etc).
- Form a prayer list to use daily or weekly and revise it often.
- Begin your prayertime with thanksgiving and praise.
- Pray for yourself (personal petitions) and on behalf of others (intercession).
- Pray the Scriptures especially when words fail you.
- Conclude your prayer with confidence that God will answer.

Sometimes your prayer life will be strengthened by a new procedure.

On a recent missions trip, I learned the power of prayerwalking. While I have often prayed as I walked, I never fully understood how to intentionally prayerwalk. That experience has enriched my prayer life. Prayerwalking is a procedure for prayer used by Christians around the world to experience prayer on location. The idea is to use the five senses—sight, hearing, smell, taste, and touch—to increase the intercessor's understanding of prayer needs. Try it! Prayerwalk your neighborhood asking God to make you sensitive to the sights and sounds and smells around you. Your passion for prayer will be strengthened as you understand the needs.

Have you recently discovered a new procedure for prayer? How has it strengthened you?

_____

_____

_____

Witnessing is a challenging spiritual discipline for many Christians. Most of us are hesitant to witness—we are paralyzed by fear. We often believe that someone else has been gifted in evangelism or is more equipped to witness.

My husband, who is an evangelism professor, says, "All Christians think evangelism is a very important task—for someone else to do." How sad, but true! We must discipline ourselves to share our faith with others. The Bible says, *"For God did not give us a spirit of timidity, but a spirit of power, of love and of self-discipline"* (2 Timothy 1:7 NIV). The power of the witness comes from God and works through a believer who is disciplined.

A lifestyle example plus a verbal witness are essential tools for evangelism. It is not enough to live a good life. We must also be willing to speak a word about Jesus. The Bible says, *"Always be ready to give a defense to anyone who asks you for a reason for the hope that is in you. However, do this with gentleness and respect, keeping your conscience clear"* (1 Peter 3:15-16). Discipline in preparation is required to be ready as a witness.

My dad is an evangelist—a bold witness. My husband is an evangelism professor—an expert in the field. It seems so easy for them to witness. But even they must be determined to regularly share their faith. I must work hard in the area of witnessing. I don't feel gifted or qualified as a witness. God honors my desire and my determination. Several years ago I asked my husband to write a simple tract for me to use in witnessing. He wrote a thank-you note that included a simple plan of salvation. I can confidently use this tool to begin a conversation about the Lord with a waitress or clerk or bellman. I have learned that I can witness in His power, but I had to decide to do it.

Spiritual discipline is necessary for Christian growth. Daily self-control must be exerted in order to mature in the faith. In the book *Control Yourself! Practicing the Art of Self-Discipline*, by D. G. Kehl, Richard Halverson said: "There is discipline involved in Christian growth. The rapidity with which a man grows spiritually and the extent to which he grows depends upon this discipline."

It is the discipline of the means. Spiritual discipline through Bible study, prayer, and witnessing is just the first step in the process of maturity. A Christian must also practice the spiritual disciplines of service, worship, solitude, simplicity, and others in order to become more like Christ. Personal discipline and mental discipline must also be developed by the believer.

Personal Discipline

The disciplines of life impact your spiritual condition and your personal life. Daily discipline is needed for self-improvement and personal achievement. To be honest, I'd rather not talk about personal discipline. It is my toughest challenge. Spiritual discipline seems an obvious effort for the Christian. Mental discipline is necessary for success in the world. But personal discipline seems to affect only me. That is not true! Personal discipline has a profound influence on others. I would choose to ignore it because personal discipline is so hard for me. It is difficult for me to be consistent in exercise and healthy eating. I find many excuses for my lack of discipline in fitness and nutrition. However, I do know how important they are to my overall health and energy.

Nutrition and fitness are important for many obvious reasons. For the Christian, they are an act of obedience to Christ. While outward appearance should not be the primary goal, a balanced diet and regular exercise improve overall health and increase vitality. A healthy Christian is better conditioned for service and better prepared to witness. Personal discipline makes us fit to work for the Kingdom.

There are numerous Scriptures about physical discipline. **Read the verses below and note the biblical teaching about the body.**

Psalm 139:13–18 _____

Romans 12:1 _____

1 Corinthians 6:19–20 _____

Our bodies are gifts from God (Psalm 139:13–18). As good stewards, we must care for our gifts. It will be our responsibility to give our bodies back to God as a sacrifice of love (Romans 12:1). We must glorify God in our body, which is His temple (1 Corinthians 6:19–20). Disciplined believers should dedicate their bodies to God and tend their bodies for Him.

In my book *Divine Discipline*, I included some nutrition tips and fitness helps. A summary of those tips is also included in Appendix C of this book. Some of the nutrition tips I remember include: eat smaller amounts more often; throw food away or save it for later; eat only in an eating place; and focus on healthy eating not dieting. Some of the fitness helps I remember include: vary kinds of exercise; make exercise fun; set realistic goals; and keep it up. While there are many other practices for healthy eating and proper exercise, these are a few to consider.

Now that you have read the nutrition and fitness suggestions that have been helpful to me, write below any additional strategies that have been useful to you.

My Nutrition Tips: _____

_____

My Fitness Tips: _____

_____

In addition to physical discipline, I also struggle with the discipline of my priorities. I have so much to do and so little time. My daily challenge is prioritizing my work.

A disciplined believer should order specific priorities around Jesus (Philippians 3:13–14). The one thing we should always do is spend time with Him. Many Christians lose control of their lives because Jesus is not the focus. I am constantly searching for time management strategies to help me be more productive. I have learned that I have all the time I need and I have the same amount of time as everyone else. My task is to discipline my time.

Appendix C includes "12 Timely Tips," which I introduced in *Divine Discipline*. They are simple truths about time, designed to promote personal discipline. I have found that life never gets simplier, and priorities never get easier to manage. So, learn to use your time wisely and invest in the things that matter the most.

Carefully read the "12 Timely Tips" in the back of the book and add your own suggestions in the space provided then practice them.

More Timely Tips: _____

_____

_____

Efficient control of time is critical to personal discipline.

Jesus' twelve disciples grew spiritually, but they also grew personally. Their growth didn't just happen. They had to practice divine discipline. The disciples also grew mentally. They increased their knowledge and understanding. Mental growth should be another pursuit of obedient believers. Discipline yourself *spiritually, personally*, and *mentally*.

Mental Discipline

Intellectual growth was evidenced in the life of Jesus. He who was omniscient (all-knowing) continued to learn. He expects us to grow in wisdom and knowledge too. Though many truths of God are mysteries that must be accepted by faith, there is much that can be learned. Our minds can expand as we practice mental discipline.

The Bible exhorts believers to increase in wisdom and knowledge. *Wisdom* is the power to judge rightly and follow a sound course of action. It is an acquisition based on experiences more than knowledge of facts. Wisdom is often a virtue attributed to age. In other words, wisdom comes with white hair. If only that were true! Years of experience in life provide true wisdom. God's children should seek wisdom from Him. The experience of God offers infallible wisdom.

In Psalm 51 David pled for godly wisdom: *"God, create a clean heart for me and renew a steadfast spirit within me"* (Psalm 51:10). His song asking for forgiveness was also a plea for wisdom to make important decisions and live a righteous life. Isaiah prophesied of the Messiah's infinite wisdom in Isaiah 11:2 — *"The Spirit of the Lord will rest upon Him — a Spirit of wisdom and understanding."* The Old Testament also includes wisdom literature (Job, Proverbs, Ecclesiastes, and selected Psalms). These Scriptures give practical advice and contrast wise and foolish choices.

The New Testament also teaches about wisdom. Paul frequently encouraged believers to seek wisdom from God. In Ephesians 1:17, Paul prayed for his fellow Christians that God *"would give you a spirit of wisdom and revelation in the knowledge of Him."* He acknowledged wisdom as a spiritual gift in 1 Corinthians 12 — *"There are diversities of gifts...to one is given the word of wisdom"* (1 Corinthians 12:4, 8 NKJV). In Colossians, Paul professed that wisdom could be received from the Lord and was necessary to know God's will.

Find Colossians 1:9–10 in your Bible then read the passage carefully. Why is wisdom essential to the Christian life?

_____

_____

Paul prayed that God would give wisdom and spiritual understanding to the believers so they could walk worthy of the Lord, please Him, be fruitful, and increase in knowledge. Wisdom is available to you if you ask for it by faith: *"Now if any of you lacks wisdom, he should ask God, who gives to all generously and without criticizing, and it will be given to him"* (James 1:5). God gives wisdom and He gives it generously.

I am grateful for the wise counsel of older Christian friends. Early in my ministry, God used an elderly woman named Mrs. Seaman to share godly advice with me. This 92-year-old saint made a thoughtful suggestion that improved the way I led a prayer group. When we spent all our allotted time discussing prayer requests and not praying, she loaned me a book by Rosalind Rinker, *Prayer: Conversing with God.* As I read the book, God taught me that we need to spend more time talking *to* Him than *about* Him. God used the wisdom of a 92-year-old woman to teach me about prayer. Christians should spend more time praying than talking about prayer.

Proverbs 4:5 exhorts the reader to acquire wisdom and knowledge. *Knowledge* is the accumulation of information and learning. In contrast to the experience of wisdom, knowledge must be taught. Both characteristics describe Jesus and His disciples. Faithful followers must increase in wisdom and develop knowledge. The knowledge of God is wonderful and difficult to attain (Psalm 139:6). Knowledge is a godly virtue that helps God's children control their tongues and their tempers (Proverbs 17:27). Though knowledge should be sought, the love of Christ *"surpasses knowledge"* (Ephesians 3:19).

At times I feel knowledgeable. After all, I do have 25 years of formal education! But there are times that I don't feel very smart. Books don't teach everything. Information read in books may help you carry on a good conversation, but many important things are learned only through experience. God desires for us to accrue wisdom as well as knowledge.

Consider for a moment the difference between wisdom and knowledge. How are they different? And why are they important? Express your thoughts here.

_____

_____

_____

Mental growth results when the mind is disciplined. Reading, studying, learning, and understanding stimulate the believer to grow and improve. Wisdom and knowledge are attributes of God and should be virtues of His children.

During our seminary graduations, our provost Dr. Steve Lemke, reminds the graduates that while they have learned a lot during their years of training that they don't know everything. Much is learned through the school of experience. In fact, the more you learn, the more you realize you do not know. So mental discipline is a life process.

Paul rejoiced in the wisdom and knowledge of God in Romans 11:33–36:

> *"Oh, the depth of the riches both of the wisdom and knowledge of God! How unsearchable His judgments and untraceable His ways! For who has known the mind of the Lord? Or who has been His counselor? Or who has ever first given to Him, and has to be repaid? For from Him and through Him and to Him are all things. To Him be glory forever. Amen."*

Discipline is needed in all areas of life—spiritual, personal, and mental. Without discipline, there is no growth. Where there is no growth, there is death. Growth in only some areas leads to imbalance. God wants His children to be healthy, mature, and balanced spiritually, personally, and mentally. Paul often taught young Christians like Timothy and Titus the importance of divine discipline.

Read 1 Timothy 4:7–8 then summarize the advice of Paul.

_____

_____

_____

All of us should heed Paul's words of wisdom to young Timothy: *"Discipline yourself for the purpose of godliness; for bodily discipline is only of little profit, but godliness is profitable for all things, since it holds promise for the present life and also for the life to come"* (1 Timothy 4:7–8 NASB).

Discipline has immediate earthly benefits, but it also brings infinite eternal blessings. The original disciples provide models of growth and maturity for us today. Those followers of Christ disciplined themselves in their daily lives in order to experience spiritual maturity, personal development, and mental growth necessary to serve the Lord. As contemporary Christians, we, too, should develop and maintain self-control. If we profess Christ as Savior and serve Him as Lord, we must practice divine discipline until He returns.

My Personal Discipline

How disciplined are you in these areas—spiritual, personal, and mental? After you honestly evaluate yourself, set some goals for growth and list them below.

Spiritual Growth

1. _____

2. _____

3. _____

Personal Growth

1. _____

2. _____

3. _____

Mental Growth

1. _____

2. _____

3. _____

Dear Lord:
Thank You for Your strength and guidance in the search for divine discipline. Help me develop and maintain spiritual maturity, personal development, and mental growth. Then I will be ready to share the message of self-discipline with others. Amen.

Lesson 12
Self-Control and Others

Divine Instruction

Encourage the young women to love their husbands and to love their children, to be self-controlled, pure, homemakers, kind, and submissive to their husbands, so that God's message will not be slandered. — Titus 2:4–5

All of us would agree that we live in an undisciplined world. The people around us and we ourselves lack discipline in many areas of life. It is easy to see the faults of others as well as our own weaknesses. Violence has risen. Sexual immorality is rampant. Health problems are raging. These excesses are the result of little discipline in our society. Just recently my hometown of New Orleans was voted the "fattest city in America." We are proud of our delicious food, and we are undisciplined in our eating. Lack of self-control has become epidemic in proportion.

It is time that we focus on our own self-control and recognize that we cannot control others. However, it is encouraging to know that our disciplined lives can influence others to godliness. As we grow through discipline, our righteousness can rub off on them. Through us, God can change the world!

The influence people can have on others is an acknowledged fact. Children can be positively or negatively influenced by their peers. Adults can also be impacted by others. Their words of counsel and lives of example can help determine how a person lives. In recent years, the process of personal influence has been described as mentoring. The power of mentoring is great. A person who shares her life experiences with another can greatly affect others. Mentoring is one way we can teach self-control to others.

Are you familiar with the term *mentoring*? What do you understand mentoring to be?

_____

_____

_____

Technically, mentoring is "the process of tutoring or coaching" (*Merriam-Webster's*). Relationally, mentoring is mutual encouragement between two people. In her book *A Garden Path to Mentoring*, Esther Burroughs described mentoring as "planting your life in another and releasing the fragrance of Christ."

I love the visual description of mentoring with one hand holding an older woman who has gone before you and one hand holding on to a younger woman coming after you. At all times we should both be mentored and be mentoring. How wonderful to know that our disciplined life can be a godly influence on others.

The Bible challenges women to train other women through their Christian example. **Read what Paul has to say about mentoring in Titus 2:1–5. After reading the passage, fill in the blanks below. Women should teach other women...**

to _____ their husbands
to _____ their children
to be _____
to be _____
to be _____
to be _____
to be _____ to their own husbands

The Bible instructs Christians to teach others to live godly lives, to be disciplined. Paul specifically encouraged godly women to teach other women by example and words to love their husbands and children, to be good homemakers, to be self-disciplined as well as pure, kind, and submissive to their husbands. We have not only been commanded to train others, we have been given specific guidelines for the training. Christian women need to be busy pouring themselves into the lives of other women so they can lead them into godliness.

As we share what God has taught us with others, the Lord is glorified and His Word is proclaimed. **Who has influenced your life? What women have helped you as they have shared their life experiences with you? List their names below and thank the Lord for their positive influence on you.**

_____

_____

More importantly, whose lives have you influenced? Has God brought women into your life for you to mentor? If so, list their names below.

_____

_____

I am so very grateful for the many younger women that God puts into my life as I teach at New Orleans Baptist Theological Seminary. It is a privilege to encourage them and then to see them grow into the women God created them to be. God chooses to teach us things so that we can be changed, and then we can influence others to change. Self-discipline should be learned so that it can be shared.

In this final lesson, we will investigate how we can share our personal discipline with others. The only way we can do that is through the power of the Holy Spirit. If God empowers our discipline, it will overflow into the lives of others. If we depend on ourselves for discipline, there will be little lasting impact on ourselves or others.

Some would say that we should be able to obtain self-control in our own strength. I have tried repeatedly and have failed every time. It is impossible for any individual to maintain self-control in human power alone. Human effort is limited and superficial. We may achieve momentary discipline, but in time we return to our insufficient, sinful ways. However, as believers we can claim the supernatural power of God to maintain divine discipline. The key to maintaining self-control is yielding control of the self to the Holy Spirit. Self-control is possible! Then self-control can be shared with others as we build them up, lift them up, and train them up.

Build Them Up!

The Bible clearly teaches Christians that we are to encourage one another. In the same way that the affirmation of others helps us develop divine discipline, our positive words can build self-control in others. One of the strongest themes of the Book of Ephesians is relationships with others. In Chapter 4, Paul describes how godly people should interact with one another in love.

At this time, read Ephesians 4:25–32 to understand how disciplined Christians are to encourage each other. In the space below, summarize how we should speak to others.

_____

_____

_____

Believers are always to speak the truth (v. 25). Our speech should not be in anger (v. 26). We should never let any ungodly or demeaning words come out of our mouths. Paul said it this way *"No foul language is to come from your mouth, but only what is good for building up someone in need, so that it gives grace to those who hear"* (Ephesians 4:29). Our words should literally build a person up—they should be like grace gifts.

In her book *Silver Boxes*, Florence Littauer reinforces the tremendous power in a word. She expressed her interpretation of Ephesians 4:29 like this: "Our words should be gifts to each other, little silver boxes with bows on top." She taught this biblical principle to her children and we can teach it to others. Our words have the power to build people up or tear them down. With divine discipline, we can always speak words of love and concern.

As women, wives, mothers, sisters, daughters, and friends, we have many opportunities to strengthen others as we speak words of encouragement. But we must also discipline our tongues to not be critical or negative or judgmental. **Consider your own speech. Do you typically speak words of kindness or do you often speak unkindly? Think of those loved ones who need your words of encouragement. Write at least five statements below that will build them up.**

1. _____

2. _____

3. _____

4. _____

5. _____

During the recent Christmas holidays, I have tried to practice giving words of encouragement not just presents. My family gathered in our home, and we had such sweet fellowship. I spoke these statements with the desire to build up each member of my family. To my husband I said, "I am so grateful that you love my family like your own." To my parents I said, "Thank you for providing my wonderful education." To my sister I said, "You bring such joy to my life." To my nephews I said, "I am proud of the young men you are becoming." What a privilege to be an encourager to others.

It has been said that "it takes five compliments to erase a criticism." How true! We remember unkind comments for a long time. Many kind words are needed to remove negative impressions. Charles Swindoll calls discouragement "the devil's calling card." The devil loves it when the Christian speaks painful words. The Lord smiles when we speak words of love. Encouragement must be God's calling card — He wants us to share His love with others.

What are some specific ways your words can build others up? Begin by eliminating negative critical words from your vocabulary. I try not to use the word "problem" because this charged word immediately puts the listener on the defensive, thinking the worst about the situation. Replace those ungodly words with positive, loving words. Listen to yourself as you speak. Eliminate your undesirable vocabulary. Also, look for ways to praise other people. See beyond their faults and recognize their strengths. Sometimes you may have to look deeply, but everyone has a strength. A friend said her mother-in-law always had something good to say about everyone. This godly woman even had something good to say about the devil—"he works very hard." What a precious encourager!

If we want to change the world, we must use divine discipline to build each other up. Our human natures are much more prone to tear each other down. Critical words and bitter comments flow easily from our mouths. And have you noticed that bitterness is contagious? Critical people rub off on others and change the whole atmosphere around them. So we must eliminate the negative and accentuate the positive. Be a positive agent in your family, at work, in church, and in your community. Be a builder not a breaker. Our harsh, painful words can destroy a person's spirit.

While criticism is natural to us, God gives us the power to control our tongues and speak words that will encourage others. Our words can benefit and bless rather than hurt and harm. One way for your self-control to build others up is with words of encouragement. You can also lift them up and train them up.

Lift Them Up!

Divine discipline is needed to give encouragement to others. It also takes supernatural self-control to minister to those in need. As Christians, we must not be satisfied with the personal benefits of self-discipline. We must be willing to share the benefits with others. The Bible says that God *"comforts us in all our affliction, so that we may be able to comfort those who are in any kind of affliction, through the comfort we ourselves receive from God"* (2 Corinthians 1:4). God comforts us so that we can comfort others. God lifts us up so we can lift up others! We must discipline ourselves to meet the needs of others, to minister to the lost and lonely, to lift up the down and out. God will give us the power to minister in His name.

Paul challenged the Christians in Corinth to comfort in suffering—to minister to those who were hurting. Just as God had strengthened them in their times of weakness, those Christians in turn could help others. **Read the lesson of Paul in 2 Corinthians 1:3–7, then answer the following questions.**

Who is the source of help?_____

When is help offered?_____

What must those helped do? _____

What is the reward? _____

What is the hope? _____

Since suffering is a natural part of life, there will be many opportunities to extend comfort. God's mercy will comfort you in times of trouble (v. 3). He will offer comfort at *all* times and in *all* types of suffering (v. 4). God expects His children to then comfort others (v. 4). To the prophet Isaiah, God said, *"comfort My people!"* (Isaiah 40:1). He expects His children today to care for others. Then the gracious Lord blesses those who bless others (v. 6). He gives hope in despair and strength in suffering (v. 7).

God is at work today in the lives of women. He is using women to reach out to other women, to build up and lift up. Many churches are organizing women's ministries not just to plan events or sponsor programs. A women's ministry can minister personally to women in the church and community who are hurting. Such ministries can offer support groups and provide lay counseling. God can use the church and His children to lift up others.

Does your church have an organized women's ministry? Are the women in your church reaching out to others? If so, praise the Lord and keep up the good work! You can join God in His work through women's ministry. If not, you can be used by God individually to minister to women in need or help start a women's ministry in your own church.

What are some of the needs of women you know? Think about general needs of most women and specific needs of a particular woman. List your observations below.

General Needs	Specific Needs

Discipline is necessary to even notice the needs of others, much less take action to do something about them. You must look beyond yourself and see those hurting around you. Then you must do something about it. I pray that some of the following suggestions will help you reach out to women who are hurting and lift them up in the name of Jesus.

- Start a small prayer group with other concerned women and pray specifically for those in need within your fellowship.
- Find someone who has a similar challenging life experience to yours and explain how God has strengthened you.
- Find one woman with a special need and minister to her, discipling her spiritual growth.
- Ask a new Christian to be your Bible study partner; meet regularly to study the Scriptures and discuss their meaning.
- Form a small support group of women with a common challenge and discuss biblical solutions.
- Open your home to those in need of hospitality and fellowship. God will bless you as you reach out to others in His name.

Disciplined believers will serve others.

Jesus, our perfect example, served others; so should we. Jesus Himself said that He *"did not come to be served, but to serve, and to give His life—a ransom for many"* (Matthew 20:28). Service is ministering in love to the needs of others. The local church is the best context for service. Many programs in the church offer opportunities for ministry to others. **What opportunities for service does your church offer? List these ministries briefly.**

I am so grateful that my church has many ministry programs. Each Wednesday night many members go out into our community with a Care Effect Ministry, feeding the homeless, tutoring school children, leading Bible studies in a juvenile center, and teaching English as a second language. My mother faithfully delivers food to the homebound each week and encourages them. She is a blessing to those she serves, but she also receives a blessing from her service. Many have been ministered to both physically and spiritually. Every believer should be involved in specific ministry.

God wants all of His children to be encouragers and servants. He wants us to comfort others in His name. He will supply our needs so that we can reach out to others. There are many ways for us to change the world, but first we must be committed to the task and disciplined to do it. God wants to *build people up*, *lift people up*, and *train people up*!

Train Them Up!

I do pray that you agree that others can be influenced by our personal discipline. As we learn self-control, we can teach it to others.

Build them up! Lift them up! Train them up! God desires to work through us to teach His children life-changing lessons. Even those who are willing to grow must be trained to do it. One of the most effective ways to share your self-control with others is to teach them through words and actions about divine discipline. Invite them to live life alongside of you.

It is such a joy for me to train women's ministry leaders. I was blessed by the instruction of many, and now I can teach others. I learned to teach Bible studies by co-leading a small group with my mentor, JoAnn Leavell. I learned about public speaking from dear friends like Esther Burroughs and Marge Caldwell. I learned about writing from many Christian authors like Anne Ortlund and Elisabeth Elliot. God has placed gifted women in my life to teach me. Now I can teach others. And I must say that there is no greater joy than seeing God work in a mighty way through the ministry of a student. In recent months, three of my women's ministry students have published first books. What a thrill to write endorsements for their works. I feel like a proud mama!

Paul the Apostle was grateful for his Spirit-given ability to teach and preach the gospel. He was also ready to share all that he had learned with young ministers. In his first letter to Timothy, Paul challenged all of us to train others in the faith. **Read 1 Timothy 4:12–16 carefully.**

In what ways are Christians to teach others? _____

_____

_____

What should not be neglected? _____

_____

_____

What happens when you continue in the faith? _____

_____

_____

The biblical mandate is clear — "Be an example!" Christians are to teach others in word, in conduct, in love, in spirit, in faith, and in purity (v. 12). Disciplined reading and study is necessary to teach the truth (v. 13). Gifts of ministry should never be neglected (v. 14). Total commitment and unselfish service must continue all the days of your life — then both you and others will be blessed.

What kind of teacher are you? Are you training others in personal discipline? Evaluate your instruction of others. Are you an excellent, satisfactory, or unsatisfactory example to them?

Check your honest answer below.

	Excellent	Satisfactory	Unsatisfactory
My words	_____	_____	_____
My conduct	_____	_____	_____
My love	_____	_____	_____
My spirit	_____	_____	_____
My faith	_____	_____	_____
My purity	_____	_____	_____

With divine discipline, your influence will be strengthened. You can be used by God to train others for service to Him.

Proverbs 22:6 is not only a challenge for parents but a promise as well. It is a conditional promise for spiritual parents as well as biological parents. Whether or not you gave birth to the child, you are to *"teach a youth about the way he should go; even when he is old he will not depart from it."* Parenting is an awesome responsibility demanding daily self-control. We can be confident that if we teach our children the important things of God, they will not forsake His teachings. Though our children may turn away from the Lord and even their parents, what an assurance to know that our training will not leave them. As parents we need to discipline but also to encourage *self-discipline*.

As Christians, we must train others to be controlled. Instruction in discipline is the most profound influence we can have on another person. What a privilege and a responsibility to share with others what we have learned about self-discipline! We are blessed and they are blessed as we build them up, lift them up, and train them up.

Now that you have learned the lesson of divine discipline, it is your responsibility to teach it to others. As God changes your life, He will change others through you. Your world may include a husband, children, family, friends, neighbors, or customers. Each of them needs to see your example of self-control and hear your message of divine discipline. With the help of the Lord, you can share His truth and meet real-life needs. Persevere as you encourage, minister to, and train others.

Some of them will be slow learners—slow to learn the things of God. You must be patient with them and continue your work. If you constantly build them up, lift them up, and train them up, God will use you to influence their lives. Nothing is more rewarding than to see spiritual growth in a young Christian you disciple. There are many precious blessings as you train others to be self-controlled. There are great rewards in living a disciplined life!

My Personal Discipline

How effectively are you training others in divine discipline? Think about your own children or some spiritual children. Are they learning to be disciplined from you? Write their names below then identify an area of discipline you can teach them.

Name	Lesson
_____	_____
_____	_____
_____	_____

Dear Lord:
I do want my divine discipline to be an influence. Help me to build others up through encouragement, lift them up through ministry, and train them up through the lesson of divine discipline. Amen.

Conclusion

Today is another day—another day of discipline. In fact, only those days committed to personal discipline will be days of faithfulness and obedience. That truth has been the most significant lesson I have learned about self-control. Daily recommitment is required for a disciplined life. Have you learned that lesson? Have you made that commitment? It is my prayer that this Bible study has encouraged your pursuit of personal discipline.

This journey of divine discipline has been life changing for me. I pray it has been life-changing for you. We began our study by exploring why personal discipline is important. It is necessary for personal development, spiritual growth, and Christian service. We also discussed the essence of discipline from the secular, biblical, and personal perspectives. At its core, self-discipline is a learned behavior God wants to teach every believer—a godly behavior that can impact all areas of life.

Each one of us has passions, feelings, and temperaments that must be disciplined with the help of the Holy Spirit. We must avoid unrighteousness, engage in holiness, and purpose for godliness. But personal discipline is not easy. It is possible only with determination and divine intervention.

The first step toward discipline is personal willpower. Each individual must make a genuine commitment, create ideal conditions, and maintain lifestyle changes. Then as a second step the believer can seek supernatural Godpower, which is truly divine discipline. Strength for personal discipline is received through His presence, His power, and His joy. The third step in the development of discipline is accepting people's persuasive power. Other people offer acceptance, affirmation, and accountability in your personal pursuit. Personalization is essential to lasting discipline. Each person must identify weaknesses of character, set goals for development, and reward accomplishments with praise. A final step in the process is perseverance. Discipline must continue with patience, persistence, and permanence throughout life.

Though discipline at first is painful, it does have its eventual rewards. As discipline is practiced, the believer experiences past blessing, present freedom, and future hope. Self-control also influences other disciplines including spiritual, personal, and mental. All areas of life can be positively enhanced by divine discipline. And personal discipline can impact other people. Disciplined believers can build others up, lift others up, and train others up. Divine discipline is a personal blessing and a blessing to others.

As you begin and continue your pursuit of divine discipline, claim this biblical promise that has given me hope and persistence: *"No discipline seems pleasant at the time, but painful. Later on, however, it produces a harvest of righteousness and peace for those who have trained by it"* (Hebrews 12:11 NIV).

Though self-control will be painful and difficult at first, if you persevere in divine discipline, God will bless you richly. The disciplined believer receives not just a little blessing but an abundance of His righteousness and peace. The tough life lesson of personal discipline will positively impact all areas of your life and provide rewards beyond all measure. May God richly bless your disci-plined life!

Group Teaching Guide

This section includes some teaching suggestions for the small group leader. It also provides a format for the discussion time and a typical schedule for a one-hour session. This particular group approach has been tried successfully with a focus group. However, let the Holy Spirit lead your group discussion and make any appropriate changes. These are simply teaching helps.

LESSON 1: The Importance of Discipline

Prayertime (5 minutes)
As this study begins, encourage each group member to spend time in private prayer. Ask her to honestly talk with the Lord about her need for personal discipline. Conclude the prayertime by voicing your own commitment to discipline. Ask each person to share a personal goal for growth during the study.

Review (5 minutes)
Discuss the format for the study and the details about the group meeting. Review the schedule and encourage each member to complete her own study before discussing it with the group. Ask each person to share a personal goal for growth during the study.

Introduction (5 minutes)
Take a few minutes to discuss with the group the truth that discipline is not optional for the Christian. Though the topic is unpopular and uncomfortable, discipline must be learned by all believers. Read 1 Timothy 4:7–8 aloud and discuss its meaning.

Group Discussion (40 minutes)
1. Ask the group members to discuss why they think discipline is important. List the reasons on the board.

2. Seek a volunteer to read aloud Luke 2:52. Then discuss how Jesus disciplined Himself.
3. Allow time for the ladies to silently read Galatians 5:22–23. List the nine specific descriptors of the fruit of the Spirit on the board. Then ask the group to suggest ungodly behaviors that may result from a lack of discipline.
4. Discuss how personal discipline will help their Christian service. Conclude your discussion by reading and restating Hebrews 12:11.

Closing (5 minutes)
Provide an index card for each person. Ask them to write a prayer of commitment to personal discipline then pray the prayer aloud with another group member. Suggest that each lady keep the prayer card as a reminder of her commitment.

LESSON 2: The Essence of Discipline

Prayertime (5 minutes)
Begin your Bible study by asking the group to pray Hebrews 12:11. Have ladies prayerfully read the verse from several different translations. Conclude the prayertime by saying, "It is truly our commitment, Lord, to practice divine discipline."

Review (5 minutes)
Review lesson one by discussing why discipline is important. Ask the group members to share any new insights about personal discipline.

Introduction (5 minutes)
As you begin to define self-control, share your personal definition. Encourage the ladies to share their own definitions. Discuss common themes among them.

Group Discussion (40 minutes)
1. Ask the group members to read aloud several of the definitions of self-control they found during their research. Have them cite their sources.
2. Provide several Bible resources, including a Bible dictionary, concordance, and commentary, and ask individuals to read biblical

definitions of self-control. They may choose to share from their homework.
3. Read Titus 2:11–14 and ask the group members to discuss what the Scripture means personally.
4. As the study concludes, allow time for the group to complete "My Personal Discipline." Encourage them to honestly explain

Closing (5 minutes)
Ask the ladies to silently pray for the woman seated to her right. Suggest that they pray specifically for her daily commitment to divine discipline. Continue praying for her throughout the week.

LESSON 3: Outward Offenses and Discipline

Prayertime (5 minutes)
Share praises for how God has been working. Ask one person to voice a prayer of praise. Briefly share prayer requests, calling on one person to pray specifically. Then close in a prayer of thanks for God's answers.

Review (5 minutes)
Go around the room and ask each person to share one word or thought about what personal discipline means to her. Summarize the meaning of self-control and several of the definitions shared in the previous lesson.

Introduction (5 minutes)
Take a few minutes to discuss why outward behaviors must be disciplined. Read what Paul said in 2 Timothy 2:20–21. A disciplined life can be useful to the Master, prepared for every good work.

Group Discussion (40 minutes)
1. Read the list of ungodly outward behaviors to be disciplined in Galatians 5:19–21. Discuss them in relationship toward God, others, and self.
2. Lead the group to discuss spiritual disciplines that are difficult. Ask for helpful suggestions about each spiritual discipline.

3. Have the group read Philippians 3:13–14 together. Briefly discuss how to purpose for godliness.
4. Have one group member read aloud the ten principles for controlling outward behavior suggested by Richard Foster in *Celebration of Discipline*. Discuss them briefly.

Closing (5 minutes)
In a time of confession, ask each group member to write an outward offense on a piece of paper. Encourage them to silently confess and pray for forgiveness according to 1 John 1:9. Then tell them to wad the paper up and throw it away. God forgives us of our sins.

LESSON 4: Inward Instincts and Discipline

Prayertime (5 minutes)
Begin the Bible study with sentence prayers. Ask a volunteer to pray specifically for one classmate to be committed to divine discipline. Then encourage other members to pray for another individual. The leader should close the prayer.

Review (5 minutes)
Remind the group that discipline of outward behaviors is essential in the life of a believer. Read Galatians 5:19–21 then discuss why Christians must avoid these behaviors.

Introduction (5 minutes)
Ask the group members which is harder to discipline—outward behaviors or inward instincts. Discuss why it is more difficult to discipline that area of life.

Group Discussion (40 minutes)
1. Read the definition of "passion" printed in this book. Encourage the group to honestly identify some of their personal passions.
2. Discuss why ungodly feelings grieve or hinder the work of the Holy Spirit. Read Ephesians 4:31–32 and list other ungodly behaviors that are harmful.

3. Contrast the righteous man and the wicked man in Proverbs 10:27–32. Lead the group in reading the Scripture aloud. Remind them that character matters to God.
4. Review the four personality types described in the lesson. Ask the group members to identify their personalities and explain why that type describes them best.

Closing (5 minutes)
Allow time at the end of the Bible study for members to reflect on their own personality weaknesses. Challenge them to set several specific goals to improve their weaknesses. Make a commitment in silent prayer.

LESSON 5: My Own Willpower for Discipline

Prayertime (5 minutes)
Read 2 Timothy 1:7 then encourage group members to personalize the Scripture as they pray: "Lord, you did not give me a spirit of timidity, but of power, of love and of self-discipline."

Review (5 minutes)
Ask the group to consider what they have learned about their inward selves this week—their passions, feelings, and character. Then pose the question: "Why is it important for the Christian to discipline her inner self?"

Introduction (5 minutes)
Take a few minutes to discuss willpower—what is it and why is it important? Call on someone to summarize Genesis 3:1–19, then discuss the weak willpower of Adam and Eve.

Group Discussion (40 minutes)
1. Read the parable of Jesus in Matthew 7:13–14. Discuss its meaning then ask the group what happens when people follow their own ways.
2. Ask someone in the group to read 1 Timothy 6:11–12. Spend time talking about the impact of surroundings on a person. Why is it essential for a Christian to create ideal conditions?

3. Review the five guidelines for personal discipline introduced in this lesson. Encourage the ladies to create an atmosphere of holiness.

Closing (5 minutes)
In the closing minutes, allow time for the group members to write in their books a prayer of personal commitment to divine discipline. Close the Bible study in prayer.

Lesson 6: Supernatural Godpower for Discipline

Prayertime (5 minutes)
As you begin the prayertime, ask the group members to identify an attribute of God (holy, loving, merciful, kind, forgiving). Call on one lady to voice a prayer of praise for who God is and a second one to praise God for what He has done.

Review (5 minutes)
Remind the group members that personal willpower is the first step toward divine discipline. An individual must make a personal commitment, create ideal conditions, and sustain lifestyle changes. Ask them if they are developing personal willpower.

Introduction (5 minutes)
Discuss the supernatural power of God—He is able to do what I cannot do. Ask someone to read 2 Corinthians 12:9–10. Allow time for the ladies to personalize this verse as printed in the book. Call on one volunteer to read her paraphrase aloud. Reinforce that God's grace is sufficient when we are weak.

Group Discussion (40 minutes)
1. Assign the seven different Scriptures about the presence of God to seven ladies. Ask them to summarize what they teach about the presence of God. Briefly discuss how to practice the presence of God.
2. Discuss the meaning of the word *sovereign*. Ask the group, "How does God demonstrate His power in your life?"
3. Lead the group in a discussion about spiritual joy. Contrast true joy with carnal pleasures.

4. Enlist a volunteer to read aloud Philippians 4:8–9. Then list on the board: Things to Think, Things to Do, and Things to Receive. Encourage the ladies to suggest ways for the Holy Spirit to work. Conclude by reading the quote by Anne Ortlund about the Holy Spirit's work.

Closing (5 minutes)
Read aloud 1 Corinthians 10:13 then pray for the ladies this week — that God will strengthen them to withstand all temptation.

LESSON 7: People's Persuasive Power for Discipline

Prayertime (5 minutes)
Open your Bible study with a time of silent prayer. Guide the ladies in praying for others. Suggest that they pray specifically for immediate family then extended family then friends then neighbors and finally co-workers. Remind them that there is power in praying for others.

Review (5 minutes)
Ask the group members how they have experienced supernatural Godpower this week. Remind them about practicing His presence, claiming His power, and seeking His joy.

Introduction (5 minutes)
Begin the study by asking the ladies what impact other people have on their lives. Ask them to identify women in the Bible or women in the world who have influenced them for godliness.

Group Discussion (40 minutes)
1. Ask a volunteer to read aloud John 8:1–12 then discuss the acceptance of Jesus. Then ask the group why acceptance is important for the Christian.
2. Lead the group in reading in unison 1 Thessalonians 5:12–15 as printed in the book. Then discuss why it is good to encourage others and how you encourage them.
3. Discuss accountability—what is it, why is it necessary, and how is it given. Ask group members to share areas of their lives that are strengthened by accountability.

4. Call on several of the ladies to read their paraphrases of Ephesians 4:29 then read the verse from the Bible. Discuss briefly what it means.

Closing (5 minutes)
Take the time to go around the room and have each group member identify one personal prayer request. Call on one person to voice a closing prayer for each lady then encourage the group to pray for each other all week.

LESSON 8: Personalized Discipline

Prayertime (5 minutes)
During the prayertime, focus on the Scripture—1 Peter 2:9–10. Read the passage prayerfully then ask group members to voice a praise for who they are in Christ.

Review (5 minutes)
Take a few minutes to review the power of people—their acceptance, affirmation, and accountability. Ask the group members to share ways other people have strengthened them this week.

Introduction (5 minutes)
Introduce this session by discussing how the Lord personalizes His relationship with each person—personal conversion, personal call, personal commitment. Emphasize that you can't live another person's life or fulfill their ministries.

Group Discussion (40 minutes)
1. Ask one group member to read Ephesians 4:17–24. Lead the group in listing on the board "Weaknesses of the Old Man" and "Strengths of the New Man." Then suggest that ladies identify their own weaknesses so they can overcome them with the help of the Lord.
2. Summarize for the group why it is helpful to set personal goals for discipline. Ask a volunteer to read aloud the guidelines for goal setting in the book.

3. Identify the different crowns awarded by the Lord to faithful believers. Discuss what crowns are and what they represent.
4. Read Luke 9:23 then ask the group to find the three D's necessary for personalized discipline. Remind them of the rewards of accomplishments.

Closing (5 minutes)
Allow time at the end of the session for each person to set some personal goals for discipline. Encourage them to commit those goals to the Lord in a private closing prayer.

LESSON 9: Perseverance in Discipline for a Lifetime

Prayertime (5 minutes)
Identify the lady in the group who has been a believer for the longest period of time. Enlist her to lead the opening prayer thanking God for those who have been faithful through the years.

Review (5 minutes)
Ask the group to discuss ways they have personalized their discipline this week. What specific goals have they been able to fulfill because of personal discipline? Encourage them to persevere.

Introduction (5 minutes)
Begin this week's discussion by reading several definitions of the word "perseverance." Briefly discuss what perseverance means to the Christian.

Group Discussion (40 minutes)
1. Call on one group member to read aloud 2 Peter 1:5–11. Have the group identify the virtues that must be added to faith.
2. Read James 1:2–4 then discuss what the Bible teaches about trials. Remind the ladies that patience is a product of persevering through trials.
3. Seek three volunteers to read Revelation 2:2–3; Revelation 2:19; and Revelation 3:10. Explain the praise for these churches that persisted in the faith.

4. Discuss some personal behaviors that must be changed permanently. Then lead the group in reading aloud 1 Corinthians 15:58.

Closing (5 minutes)
Ask each lady to pray this prayer of commitment — *"Help me, Lord, persevere in discipline all the days of my life."* As each person voices that prayer, it will reinforce the need to continue in personal discipline.

Lesson 10: Self-Control and the Rewards of Discipline

Prayertime (5 minutes)
During this prayertime, allow an opportunity for the ladies to reflect on the blessings of God. Ask them to voice a prayer of thanks as they feel led. Then, close the prayertime with gratitude for God's blessings.

Review (5 minutes)
Read this key Scripture verse from the last session — 1 Corinthians 15:58. Ask the group why perseverance is so important in the Christian's life.

Introduction (5 minutes)
Begin this lesson by discussing the promises of God. What is a promise? What are some of God's promises to His children? Have one person read 2 Peter 1:4.

Group Discussion (40 minutes)
1. Write on the board the titles for three columns — Past Blessing, Present Freedom, and Future Hope. Throughout this study, ask the group members to list their rewards from God for personal discipline.
2. Enlist a person to read Galatians 5:22–23. As you identify the fruit of the Holy Spirit, describe it. Discuss how these blessings relate to God, others, and self.
3. Read the four purposes of freedom as suggested by John MacArthur. Then discuss the blessing of freedom.
4. Have someone read Galatians 6:8–9 then summarize what the Bible says about future rewards. Conclude with a discussion about the crowns received by believers for faithfulness.

Closing (5 minutes)
Ask one of the ladies to read Psalm 103:1–5 as a closing prayer.

LESSON 11: Self-Control and Other Disciplines

Prayertime (5 minutes)
Take a few moments today to share personal praise and specific prayer requests. Ask one group member to pray remembering each petition.

Review (5 minutes)
Remind the group of the rewards of personal discipline — past blessings, present freedom, and future hope. Read 1 Corinthians 9:25 as a reminder of the crowns of obedience.

Introduction (5 minutes)
Discuss the importance of balance in a person's life. Draw a circle on the board and divide it into three parts. Label each part — Spiritual Discipline, Personal Discipline, and Mental Discipline. Challenge the ladies to be disciplined in all areas of life.

Group Discussion (40 minutes)
1. Spend a few minutes discussing spiritual disciplines. Then ask the ladies to share specific helps for the disciplines of Bible study, prayer, witnessing, and service.
2. Summarize what the Bible teaches about the discipline of the body. Ask the ladies to share their nutrition and fitness tips as well as their time management tips.
3. Ask someone to read Colossians 1:9–10 then discuss the difference between wisdom and knowledge.
4. Read 1 Timothy 4:7–8 and discuss why discipline is necessary for all areas of life.

Closing (5 minutes)
Allow time at the end of the study for the ladies to set some goals for personal growth and pray about them.

LESSON 12: Self-Control and Others

Prayertime (5 minutes)
During this prayertime, ask the ladies to remember those people who have influenced them. Thank God for their godly lives. Then reflect on those people who are being influenced by you. Pray for those people.

Review (5 minutes)
Review the importance of balance in a person's life. Ask the group what happens when one area of a person's life is undisciplined. Conclude by clarifying that a person is unbalanced if even one aspect of life is undisciplined.

Introduction (5 minutes)
Begin today's study with a discussion of mentoring. What is mentoring? Why is it important? Then read Titus 2:4–5 as a reminder of an older woman's responsibility to train the younger women in the Lord.

Group Discussion (40 minutes)
1. Read Ephesians 4:25–32. Ask the group how believers can build others up. Be specific.
2. Discuss some of the general needs and specific needs of women today. Then suggest some ways to meet those needs and lift the women up.
3. Remind the ladies that training in ministry is essential. Have someone read 1 Timothy 4:12–16 then discuss what must be taught to others.
4. Encourage each lady to identify several people they can mentor. Think of specific disciplines they can share with each one.

Closing (5 minutes)
In conclusion, read Hebrews 12:11. Then pray specifically by name for each lady in the group that she will persevere in personal discipline and receive a harvest of blessings.

Bibliography

Adams, Chris. *Women Reaching Women*. Nashville: LifeWay, 1997.

Adams, Jay. *Godliness Through Discipline*. Grand Rapids: Baker Book House, 1972.

Anderson, Ann Kiemel. *I'm Out to Change My World*. Grand Rapids: Zondervan, 1982.

Backus, William. *Finding the Freedom of Self-Control*. Bloomington, MN: Bethany House, 1987.

Barnes, Emilie. *Things Happen When Women Care*. Eugene, OR: Harvest House, 1990.

Bridges, Jerry. *The Practice of Godliness*. Colorado Springs: NavPress, 1983.

Bunyan, John. *The Pilgrim's Progress*. New York: Airmont, 1969.

Burroughs, Esther. *A Garden Path to Mentoring*. Birmingham: New Hope, 1997.

Cooper, Kenneth H. and Mildred. *The New Aerobics for Women*. New York: Bantam Books, 1988.

Elliott, Elisabeth. *All That Was Ever Ours*. Old Tappan, NJ: Fleming H. Revell, 1988.

Foster, Richard J. *Celebration of Discipline*. New York: Harper & Row, 1978.

Foster, Richard J. *The Challenge of the Disciplined Life: Christian Reflections on Money, Sex, and Power*. New York: Harper & Row, 1985.

Ganz, Richard. *The Secret of Self-Control*. Wheaton, IL: Crossway Books, 1998.

Hendricksen, William. *New Testament Commentary: Exposition of Galatians*. Grand Rapids: Baker Book House, 1968.

Holmes, Marjorie. *Secrets of Health, Energy, and Staying Young*. Garden City, NJ: Doubleday, 1987.

Holt, Pat and Garce Ketterman. *When You Feel Like Screaming*. Wheaton: Harold Shaw, 1988.

Hopler, Whitney. *The Fruit of the Spirit: Pursue Self-Control*. Grand Rapids: Zondervan, 2001.

Kehl, D. G. *Control Yourself! Practicing the Art of Self-Discipline*. Grand Rapids: Zondervan, 1982.

Kelley, Rhonda Harrington. *Divine Discipline: How to Develop and Maintain Self-Control*. Gretna, LA: Pelican, 1992.

LaHaye, Tim F. *Spirit-Controlled Temperament*. Wheaton: Tyndale House, 1966.

LaHaye, Tim F. *Your Temperament: Discover Its Potential*. Wheaton: Tyndale House Publishers, 1984.

Leavell, JoAnn P. *Don't Miss the Blessing*. Gretna, LA: Pelican, 1990. [Study Guide by Rhonda Harrington Kelley.]

Littauer, Florence. *Personality Plus*. Old Tappan, NJ: Fleming H. Revell, 1983.

Littauer, Florence. *Silver Boxes: The Gift of Encouragement*. Dallas: Word, 1989.

MacArthur, John F. *The MacArthur New Testament Commentary: Galatians*. Chicago: Moody, 1987.

MacDonald, Gail. *Keep Climbing*. Wheaton: Tyndale House, 1989.

MacDonald, Gordon. *Rebuilding Your Broken World*. Nashville: Oliver Nelson, 1988.

Massey, James Earl. *Spiritual Disciplines*. Grand Rapids: Francis Asbury Press, 1985.

McGinn, Linda R. *Resource Guide for Women's Ministries*. Nashville: Broadman, 1990.

Minirth, Frank, et al. *Love Hunger: Recovery from Food Addiction*. Nashville: Thomas Nelson, 1990.

Ortlund, Anne. *Disciplines of the Beautiful Woman*. Waco: Word, 1983.

Ortlund, Anne. *Disciplines of the Heart: Turning Your Inner Life to God*. Waco: Word, 1987.

Ortlund, Anne. *Discipling One Another*. Dallas: Word, 1979.

Rinker, Rosalind. *Prayer: Conversing with God*. Grand Rapids: Zondervan, 1959.

Sloan, Joanne Stuart and Cheryl Sloan Wray. *A Life That Matters: Spiritual Disciplines That Change the World*. Birmingham: New Hope, 2002.

Smith, Hannah Whitall. *The Christian's Secret of a Happy Life*. Waco: Word, 1985.

Spradlin, Marsha. *Women of Faith in the '90s*. Birmingham: New Hope, 1990.

Swindoll, Charles R. *A Quest for Character*. Portland: Multnomah Press, 1987.

Swindoll, Charles R. *Improving Your Serve*. Waco: Word, 1981.

Swindoll, Charles R. *Starting Over*. Portland, OR: Multnomah Press, 1977.

Walters, R.P. *Counseling for Problems of Self-Control*. Waco: Word, 1987.

Whitney, Donald S. *Spiritual Disciplines for the Christian Life*. Colorado Springs: NavPress, 1997.

Willard, Dallas. *The Spirit of the Disciplines*. San Francisco: Harper & Row, 1988.

Young, J. Terry. *The Spirit Within You*. Nashville: Broadman, 1977.

Appendices

Appendix A: Divine Instruction

Proverbs 12:1 — Whoever loves discipline loves knowledge.

Proverbs 13:18 — Poverty and disgrace come to those who ignore discipline.

Proverbs 15:32 — Anyone who ignores discipline despises himself.

Proverbs 23:12 — Apply yourself to discipline and listen to words of knowledge.

Proverbs 25:28 — Like a city whose walls are broken down is a man who lacks self-control. (NIV)

Acts 24:25 — Now as he spoke about righteousness, self-control, and the judgment to come, Felix became afraid.

1 Corinthians 9:25 — Now everyone who competes exercises self-control in everything.

Galatians 5:22–23 — The fruit of the Spirit is . . . self-control.

Colossians 2:5 — I (Paul) am with you in spirit, rejoicing to see your good discipline and the stability of your faith in Christ. (NASB)

1 Timothy 3:2 — An overseer, therefore, must be . . . self-controlled.

1 Timothy 3:11 — Wives, too, must be worthy of respect, not slanderers, self-controlled.

1 Timothy 4:7 — Discipline yourself for the purpose of godliness. (NASB)

2 Timothy 1:7 — God did not give us a spirit of timidity, but . . . of self-discipline. (NIV)

2 Timothy 3:1–3 — In the last days . . . people will be . . . without self-control.

Titus 1:8 — An overseer, as God's administrator, must be . . . self-controlled.

Titus 2:2 — Teach the older men to be . . . self-controlled. (NIV)

Titus 2:3–5 — Older women . . . are to teach the young women . . . to be self-controlled.

Titus 2:11–12 — The grace of God . . . teaches us . . . to live self-controlled, upright and godly lives. (NIV)

Hebrews 12:7 — Endure suffering as discipline: God is dealing with you as sons.

Hebrews 12:11 — No discipline seems enjoyable at the time, but painful.

2 Peter 1:5–7 — Supplement your faith . . . with knowledge, knowledge with self-control, self-control with endurance.

APPENDIX B: Quotations on Discipline

"Spiritual discipline is to the inner spirit what physical conditioning is to the body. The unconditioned athlete, no matter how naturally talented, cannot win a world-class race." — Gordon MacDonald

"Self-control is the power to keep oneself in check." — William Hendriksen

"Self-control is the expression of the mature life which has learned to walk with God in perfect obedience." — Terry Young

"Self-control implies a battle between a divided self." — John Piper

"Freedom is not procured by a full enjoyment of what is desired, but by controlling the desire." — Epictetus

"Self-control is the believer's wall of defense against the sinful desires that wage war against his soul. The person without self-control is easy prey for the invader." — Jerry Bridges

"The present benefit of spiritual discipline is a fulfilled, God-blessed, fruitful, and useful life."
— John MacArthur, Jr.

"Self-control is the exercise of inner strength under the direction of sound judgment that enables us to do, think, and say the things that are pleasing to God." — Jerry Bridges

"Self-control holds believers in 'bounds' not 'bonds.'" — Curt Clark

"People around us are starving for love, joy, peace, and all the other graces of the Spirit. When they find them in our lives, they know that we have something they lack — self-control." — Warren Wiersbe

"Discipline without direction is drudgery." — Donald Whitney

"The alternative to discipline is disaster." — Vance Havner

"We Protestants are an undisciplined people. Therein lies the reason for much of the dearth of spiritual insights and serious lack of moral power." — Albert Edward Day

"Self-indulgence is the enemy of gratitude, and self-discipline usually its friend and generator." — Cornelius Plantinga, Jr.

"How often do we hear about the discipline of the Christian life these days? There was a time in the Christian church when this was at the very centre, and it is, I profoundly believe, because of our neglect of this discipline that the church is in her present position." — Dr. Martyn Lloyd-Jones

"There is discipline involved in Christian growth. The rapidity with which a man grows spiritually and the extent to which he grows depends upon this discipline. It is the discipline of the means." — Richard Halverson

"True spiritual self-discipline holds believers in bounds but never in bonds; its effect is to enlarge, expand, and liberate." — D. G. Kehl

"The spiritual disciplines are not to be seen as a pretext for separation and isolation from the world. Rather they should be regarded as a means to conquest over the world." — Donald G. Bloesch

"The word *discipline* has disappeared from our minds, our mouths, our pulpits, and our culture." — Jay Adams

Nutrition Tips
1. You can control what you eat.
2. Don't let anyone love you with food.
3. Eat smaller amounts, more often.
4. Learn about foods and a balanced diet.
5. Throw food away or save it for later.
6. Choose an eating place; when eating, only eat.
7. Avoid high-sodium, high-cholesterol foods.
8. Consider more than calories; nutritional content is more important.
9. Measure success by fit of clothes, not loss of pounds.
10. Healthful eating, not dieting, is the goal.

Fitness Tips
1. There is not one best way to exercise. Find an activity that fits your interest and lifestyle.
2. Vary your type of exercise.
3. Exercise for your health, not your figure.
4. Sustained exercise for thirty minutes, three times a week, is a reasonable goal.
5. Warm up before exercise; cool down after exercise.
6. Make exercise fun and convenient.
7. Seek peer support or an exercise partner.
8. Set realistic goals; then reward your accomplishments.
9. Start!
10. Keep it up!

Timely Tips
1. You have all the time you need.
2. Plan your time or others will.
3. Leave a margin for the unexpected.
4. Do one thing at a time and finish it.
5. Learn to say no.
6. Separate the important from the urgent.
7. Use shortcuts to promote efficiency.
8. Be decisive.
9. Write it down.
10. Be time conscious.
11. Work smarter, not harder.
12. Set your course and stick to it.

New Hope® Publishers is a division of WMU®, an international organization that challenges Christian believers to understand and be radically involved in God's mission. For more information about WMU, go to www.wmu.com. More information about New Hope books may be found at www.newhopepublishers.com. New Hope books may be purchased at your local bookstore.

Use the QR reader on your smartphone to visit us online at **www.newhopepublishers.com**

If you've been blessed by this book, we would like to hear your story. The publisher and author welcome your comments and suggestions at: newhopereader@wmu.org.

Other Books in
"A Woman's Guide" Series

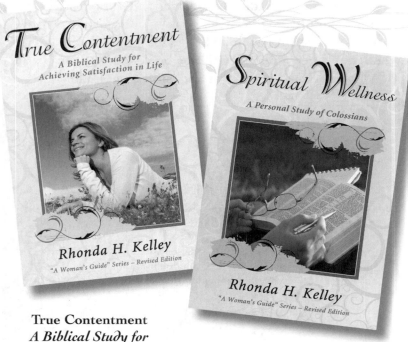

True Contentment
A Biblical Study for
Achieving Satisfaction in Life
Rhonda H. Kelley
ISBN-10: 1-59669-260-X
ISBN-13: 978-1-59669-260-2

Spiritual Wellness
A Personal Study
of Colossians
Rhonda H. Kelley
ISBN-10: 1-59669-259-6
ISBN-13: 978-1-59669-259-6

Available in bookstores
everywhere.

NEW HOPE
PUBLISHERS

For information about these books or any New Hope product,
visit www.newhopepublishers.com.